Barn

the

Spoon

SPŌN

A Guide to Spoon Carving and the New Wood Culture

Barn the Spoon

To my teachers who gave
gifts that can never be
taken away.

Introduction 9

Part One: Wood Culture

1   Trees & Woodland   31

2   The Raw Materials   43

Part Two: Knives & Axes

3   Spoon Carving Tools   61

4   Knife Grips   83

5   How to Carve a Basic Spoon   105

Part Three: The Spoons

6   Measuring Spoons   135

Caddy Spoon, Feather Spoon,
Kuksa, *Flour Scoop*

7   Cooking Spoons   157

Standard Cooking Spoon, Bent Branch Shovel,
Roma Spoon, Turned Spoon

8   Serving Spoons   181

Pouring Ladle, Salad Spoons, Bent Branch Ladle,
Sugar Spoon

9   Eating Spoons   201

Fig Shaped Spoon, Swedish Spoon, Cawl Spoon,
Dolphin Spoon

The New Wood Culture   220

Stockists & Resources   222

Introduction

Think of how many times a day you use a spoon. This simple, ordinary tool is a part of our everyday lives, intimately entwined with acts of eating and socialising, from stirring our first cup of coffee to scraping the last bit of pudding from our bowls. And who doesn't like to spoon in bed?

The spoon is the first tool we learn to use as children, and using it transports us back through human history to a time when our lives were very different, but our utensils very much the same. Using a spoon speaks of our evolution as humans, of our graduation from chips of wood – the Anglo-Saxon *spōn* – through to the beautiful Roman, Scandinavian or Celtic spoons which have inspired some of the designs you will see in this book.

Spoons are really bowls with a handle, which ask to be held, and by better appreciating our relationship with them we make our lives better. One of the things I hope this book will suggest is how much thought goes into creating something so small and apparently insubstantial as a good wooden spoon – which requires so very many things to be right to be truly good. We will celebrate the value of the tools we use, of our magnificent landscape and our key resource, the wood itself, and perhaps foremost the actions of the individual maker and his craft processes.

As a craftsperson, spoons are something upon which I have been able to build a life. Creating these small, functional sculptures has allowed me the chance to explore the concept of beauty in three dimensions, and through the process of carving using axes and knives I have discovered how satisfying making functional objects can be. I have now spent many years making spoons. I have lived in forests, learning about wood as it grows; I have been lucky enough to spend time with acknowledged experts in different aspects of woodwork, seeing how they approach their craft. All of this has left me with a great and subtle sense of a 'green wood' movement.

The definition of green wood, and green woodwork, is key to understanding the way that I create spoons. A live tree is 50 per cent water, and green wood differs from this only in so far as it is cut down, so dead, but it is still wet. Knives and axes are the key tools of the green wood worker, as they allow us to efficiently work 'wet' wood into spoons, whereas dry or 'seasoned' planks – where the water levels within the wood have reached equilibrium with their environment – tend to be worked with more industrial tools, like bandsaws and belt sanders.

Green woodwork is sympathetic to both environment and materials, and quite separate from the industrialised aspects of wood processing which only distances the individual from the tree. Green woodworkers often cut the wood themselves, or source it from tree surgeons, and the relationships we build, and the understanding of woodland practice which we acquire, has a big impact on the way we think about making spoons.

I see spoons as the emblem of, as well as the gateway to,

a broader cultural understanding; what has been called a 'new wood culture' or perhaps more appropriately a 'wood culture renaissance'. Both of these terms are about having a holistic approach to woodwork, which includes lifestyle, and about recognising that trees are fundamental to the way we have evolved as human beings. We need them to breathe, of course, but they are also central to our ideas of home and humanity – trees have given us everything from the timbers for our houses to the bows and arrows which defined our human ancestors.

The wood culture renaissance is about the rebirth of a way of life which places a sustainable interaction with trees at its centre. For woodworkers like me, it's about finding a way of working which takes a step back from machinery and puts forgotten skills back at the heart of making. Being mindful of the way we work deeply affects the physical form of our craft objects, foregrounding questions of provenance and our relationship to things we buy. These issues are pertinent today and run counter to the trend of the last century of industrialised mass production.

People have been using spoons since prehistory, with our earliest ancestors adapting horns, shells or chips of wood to help them eat. The ancient words for spoons suggest this, with the Greek and Latin word derived from *cochlea*, or spiral shell, and the Anglo-Saxon *spōn* means simply a chip of wood. Virtually all early cultures used wooden spoons to cook with and all developed their own spoon making traditions: the Shang Dynasty in China used spoons made out of bone, while the ancient Egyptians revered the wooden spoon enough to be buried with them.

The earliest known inhabitants of northern Europe were certainly woodworkers: a Neolithic stone axe found

at Ehenside tarn in Cumbria is between 5,000 and 6,000 years old. That the Iron Age Celts of Britain used spoons is evidenced by the discovery of a small wooden ladle during excavations at Glastonbury Lake Village. Despite the propensity of wooden artefacts to rot, recent discoveries have shown that Anglo Saxons and Vikings both produced wooden spoons for domestic use.

The process of carving a spoon provides a lens into a historical period when our lives were simpler and more sympathetic to the natural environment than those we lead today. The humble, rural way of life suggested by wooden spoons was largely displaced by our industrial, metropolitan age, and is considered old-fashioned at a time when we are dissatisfied with factory, but not office work – at least on the surface of things. A resurgent craft movement, recognising our need to make and do, is surely born out of the knowledge that we are not fulfilled by our sedentary, digital lives. On the fringes, people are beginning to remember the benefits of rural life, and a well-made wooden spoon, like good studio pottery before it, suggests an alternative world away from that which we currently inhabit.

The spoons I make today, however, are far from historical recreations and this is not about simply re-enacting the past. Some of them may be based, directly or indirectly, on traditional spoons found in museums but the sculptural possibilities within a craft such as spoon making are really limitless, and my aesthetic is a result of my own journey in woodwork. This includes everything from the study of ancient designs to the teachers I've learnt from, to my time tramping in the woods, to using these spoons in the kitchen. These things feed into my work in a fluid, holistic way.

Thankfully we now live in an age where the maker is resurgent, where the decision making of the craftsperson is celebrated once again. This is tied to a broader cultural renaissance. Part of this is the organic food movement, which has proved a great stimulus to the general craft enterprise, and people now care a lot more about the provenance of their purchases. The media has taken a strong interest in craft, helping to channel new feelings we have as a society as people become disenfranchised by industrialised processes. The internet has opened everything up, with a flurry of blogs providing intimate information from previously obscure makers, and given us a way to buy quality, individual and ethically sourced products.

Before the internet there were very few ways to find out about green woodwork, and no real way of learning the skills, apart from through a few specialist books, or magazines which were really designed to promote the sale of machines. Most woodworkers were approaching their material from an engineering perspective, trying to get things to within a thousandth of an inch – that was the twentieth century paradigm. But I think this processing removes all of the humanity. With industrial processes, things are either right or wrong. We have long embraced the benefits of something being well designed, but for a long time this meant designed on a drawing board, engineered, machined and mass produced, and as a result the human aspect of creation was lost.

Part of the beauty of wood as a chaotic material is that it certainly isn't ever perfectly symmetrical, on the level of the grain, and that this gives the artist something to work with, or work against. Whether it is a slight bend in the grain or a wiggle around a knot, these variables inspire sympathy in the spoon maker and an intimate relationship with their material, which is more spiritually rewarding than creating a perfect straight line or a circle.

As a child, my next door neighbour, Roger Jones, who was also my design teacher, was a proper wood worker with an inherent knowledge of wood and a drive to have a deeper relationship with it as a material. It sounds strange, but I can honestly say that I fell in love with wood at a young age. My parents got me a lathe for my thirteenth birthday and I was hooked! Whenever I carve with cherry today I am transported back to the first bowl I turned, to the curly, warm shavings being brushed from the inside of the hollow bowl and the incredible woody cherry smell that surrounded me back then. To begin with I churned out bowls and candlesticks and all sorts of weird abstract sculptures. I would wander around my school with small bits of tactile wood in my pocket, obsessing over the wood grain and the forms I was creating.

At university, I did a biology degree, which gave me the knowledge and encouraged me to think about the processes of nature and wood in action. After university I was a woodwork teacher for a while then toyed with the idea of setting up a wooden jewellery business. I was based in a dusty bedsit and using noisy machines, which started giving me breathing issues; it occurred to me that working in green wood might be the answer.

I first contacted pioneering green woodworker Mike Abbott in 2007 and went to work as an assistant on one of his chair making courses. I was living and working in the woods, cooking on an open fire each night, splitting and drying wood, and had the time and space to explore a new way of making. I was able to feel the weight of a felled tree hitting the ground and enjoy the exertion of moving tonnes of wood by hand. I soon did a whole season at Mike's, doing forestry work and helping with

In carving fresh, green wood for spoons I hope that the reader will discover trees; I hope they will discover that carving with basic edge tools, the knife and the axe, is a beautiful thing courses while working and living on the farm, helping with the apple harvest and generally doing odd jobs.

I had first made spoons during my teenage woodwork phase, but I really got into it when I was living and working at Mike's. Spoons were easy because – unlike chair making, for example – they were quick to start and something you could make around the fire at night. And yet somehow they were also the most challenging. I quickly recognised the disparity between a bad spoon and a fantastic spoon – the difference was huge and provided lots of opportunity for experiential learning on the way. Recognising that there are grades of spoons hooks you in, as there is always progress to be made.

I lived a version of the good life on this farm, with my partner, but it all fell apart; I had no money and was too old to just run back to my parents. I had been living in the woods and had no desire to change this. I had some friends who had walked the length of the country, sleeping outdoors and paying their way by playing folk music on the street, and village pubs. I decided I would do the same but with spoons.

Selling my spoons on the street taught me a lot of the sociological stuff about how to sell something you have made: how to make yourself approachable; what you should say to people; how to sit, even. Street-selling also taught me that many members of the public highly respect craftspeople, seeing them as humble, and as providing a humble service or simple product. I learned that the price you put on a spoon has nothing to do with whether it sells or not; that the average person – me included, at least to begin with – hasn't the faintest clue as to how you might price something like a handmade wooden spoon.

Recently, there was a viral video about one of the best orchestral musicians in the world who set to busking – and everybody just ignored him. It sounds slightly presumptuous, but I know how he felt. Few people have an idea about how much time and effort goes into making a wooden spoon. I was good at what I was doing, but you could tell that a lot of people who walked past me were thinking, 'Who is this tramp?' I spent a lot of time being moved on, despite having a peddler's licence. Some people offered me food; others told me to get a job. Peddlers challenge our ideas of territory, or where and how people can make a living, and our ideas of the proper boundaries of commerce. I had a lot of existential thoughts about whether people should be allowed to live in the modern world if they don't have a mortgage and a job contract.

I travelled alone for three years and it was a completely transformative journey for me. Walking for days along old ways and canal towpaths gave me time to think. I experienced life increasingly on a natural timescale, moving around on foot and stopping to gather wood for a fire, upon which I would make a cup of tea.

The most perfect time within this period was when I was living in a wood just outside Oxford, when I was able to develop a beautiful relationship with nature. After selling spoons on the city's streets I would go back to the woods. Walking through the trees at the end of the day I would find a piece of dead standing wood, or maybe a fallen branch hanging in a tree, set my tarp between branches and unravel my bed roll. This became my living room for the evening. I really had everything I needed. I'd take my shoes and socks off and sit cross-legged on my bed, then begin to process my firewood for the evening. I'd saw off nice straight bits to split into kindling, and then shave them down into feathersticks. I would light a little fire, which brought a great amount of warmth as I was so close to it and to the ground, and once the fire was really going I would reach into my pack for my metal canteen cup and water flask. I would balance the cup on the firewood, being careful not to squash the embers, and after boiling I would put a spoonful of loose leaf Earl Grey tea into it; I liked Earl Grey as it doesn't need milk, which was a hassle to carry, and you can chuck the loose leaves onto the leaf litter. I garnered a huge sense of peace in being home from a day's work. When the time came for sleep I'd pull the burning coals apart ready for the morning, and would just have to lie back to be in bed. I would sit for hours just staring into the flames. If you do this as the night encroaches your world gets smaller and smaller, finally leaving you alone under the dark canopy with only what is lit by the fire.

This was my own grounding in wood culture, an idiosyncratic and self-served apprenticeship. It taught me that it is possible to make my way in the world by selling spoons. It's a very affirming thing to make a spoon in the morning and sell it in the afternoon. It gave me an enormous sense of self respect that I could go out there with just an axe and a knife, and make a living.

In carving fresh, green wood for spoons I hope that the reader will discover trees; I hope they will discover that carving with basic edge tools, the knife and the axe, is a beautiful thing. This book will suggest that spoons are really sculptural forms, with complex angles and facets requiring both measured and instinctive cuts – and often illusions of perspective – and that spoons are as subtle, varied and valid as any other type of sculpture.

Since my days as a street-selling spoon carver, I have continued to make spoons to sell. My favourite spoons are

those which stay closest to this artisan tradition, as this inevitably has an impact upon form.

The artisan tradition involves making things quickly and efficiently – two qualities which make spoon production economically viable for a professional carver. By putting a price on their spoon, the artisan is essentially also putting a limit on how much time they can spend on a spoon. This places a premium on his skills – the faster you work the greater your empathy for the material needs to be. By simplifying the stages of production and making spoons over and over again, the artisan hones his craft; putting skill into action is what makes things interesting and enjoyable for the artisan. This time pressure encourages bold cuts, and so bold facets, which relay how the spoon was made. Each spoon thus tells its own story.

My eating spoons in particular are, in some respects, a refinement of rapidly-made original artisan forms, or historical artefacts, which are refined in so far as they have a much better finish on key areas like the rim and the inside of the bowl, but on the whole I am still beholden to the ideal of a dynamic, skilful and fast approach to your materials.

I no longer sell spoons on the street, but I still stick to the principles of the artisan. I opened a shop on the Hackney Road in Central London in 2012, providing a focal point for a newly curious public, who were impressed (and perhaps surprised) that a spoon shop even existed. It certainly raised the profile of spoons. Today, the best way to get in contact about buying spoons is through my website.

If there is a message to this book then it is that products born out of functionality, saleability and sympathy with your materials, as mine hopefully are, have a certain integrity which impacts healthily on their form. I can perhaps explain this best by previewing a handful of spoons which will feature later on in this book.

The Swedish eating spoon, for example, has a very short handle and a steep crank – crank being the angle that the handle comes into the bowl – and this combination produces a very beautiful rounded 'keel' underneath, much as you would find on a ship. But this keel is also practical because it makes the spoon very strong in use, and as carvers we take the opportunity to make this strength as elegant as possible.

Form also meets function beautifully in the feather spoon. Here the combination of a flared, flat handle with a fine, quill-like ridge creates a spoon which resembles a feather. Yet by choosing the right sort of wood – in this book the spoon is made from elm – we can add another layer to our aesthetic, and by working with the wood correctly we can bring out the striking chevrons which confirm our feather design.

When I make a spoon I am also chasing a feeling, or rather trying to communicate or prompt an emotion in a person when they pick it up. My medieval eating spoon, for example, has a fairly stretched form. It is almost as if the handle is molten glass, like it has been pinched and pulled out, and that form somehow provokes a feeling when you grasp it. This deep sense you get is almost analogous to listening to a song, where the effect may not be that obvious to begin with but, when meeting it every day, a feeling builds up over time.

This book is not a textbook, but it will provide you with a good grounding in spoon making, as I practise it in my teaching workshops. You will find helpful information on everything from buying tools to choosing the right type of wood, through to knife grips and a detailed section on how

to create your first, basic spoon. To the beginner, the technical aspects may seem a little daunting at first, but much of this information is supplemented by video tutorials on my own website.

Part three of the book builds on this acquired knowledge and is a reference work for the aspiring spoon carver, giving an insight into the methods I employ when creating sixteen of my favourite spoons. In this section I have tried to suggest something of the breadth of techniques I employ, and also the thought and craft that goes into creating some truly beautiful spoons, inspired by designs from across the world and across history. Beginners and experts alike will surely pick up some helpful hints and tips along the way. Cooks will certainly find out something about the thought which goes into the crafting of good utensils and may perhaps ask a little more from their utensils in the future. But foremost, I hope that the beginner spoon carver will be inspired to read the whole book, before buying some tools and having a go.

Part

1

Wood Culture

1

Trees & Woodland

We evolved from apes that swung in the trees to apes that swung axes at trees, and virtually all of us are descended from woodworking cultures. Spoons take us back to a time when the woods played a greater, or more obvious, role in our lives and humans worked in healthy partnership with their woodland environment. Contrast this with our more dislocated modern methods, creating fast machines requiring fossil fuels which destroy our natural habitat.

As spoon makers, we are fundamentally woodworkers, and understanding something of woodland processes allows us to better understand our materials. In Great Britain, which is where I work, 'woodland' really means a landscape shaped by thousands of years of agriculture. Unlike other countries in Europe, and the US, there aren't really any large, ancient and untouched woodlands left in the UK. Here, we have spent millennia cutting down trees for fuel, making room for our livestock and gathering materials for our industries, and certainly don't live in the kind of giant, rainforest-type ecosystem that benefits from forest fires and hurricanes – natural processes that break up the woodland canopy and create a patchwork of different habitats. Instead, for centuries we have managed our woodland, and managed to maintain something of our forests' biodiversity.

Having our landscape shaped by human activity unfortunately does not increase biodiversity, but where we have had an impact, we can do our best to promote as much diversity as possible. We have inherited different types of managed woodlands from our forebears, including much overstood coppice that could be restored to its former glory, not to mention all of the orchards and the incidental woodlands like those growing in London's abandoned Victorian cemeteries. Modern catch-all phrases like 'sustainability', 'biodiversity' and 'permaculture' are all about key aspects of appropriate woodland management, and working towards a deeper understanding of these concepts offers us an insight into the most beautiful relationship that man can have with his environment.

To my mind if you are trying to increase the amount of woodland then where possible natural regeneration makes more sense than planting. Essentially, woodlands will expand naturally and trees will grow wherever you fence out livestock. One of the largest obstacles to woodland regeneration is being gnawed upon by mammals. Trees are particularly vulnerable at a young age when livestock can still reach buds, shoots and leaves; as trees mature, the bark also becomes more resilient, or at least less tempting to opportunistic snacking. This is where the small scale use of woodland thrives: by living close to the land, and generating a diverse income from it, individuals are able to take a more holistic approach to forestry. By taking a few rabbits or deer for the pot you can keep the population in check and protect vulnerable trees whilst feeding yourself. Beyond protecting young trees, how you decide to manage the woodland is mostly down to how and when the trees are cut, and what you are trying to produce. There is huge scope for generating income for individual woodland workers whilst doing best practice for environmental reasons.

Coppicing is an ancient practice whereby an area of wood or 'copse' is harvested on rotation, which artificially creates a patchwork of diverse habitat for a diverse group of species to live in. This way of managing woodland dates back to Neolithic times, but it is still very relevant for the spoon carver today. Trees like hazel, oak, ash, sycamore and sweet chestnut sprout from the stump the year after the tree has been felled. The slim poles that begin to emerge can in time be used for things like fences, charcoal and beanpoles – and spoons. More importantly for the small scale forester, these poles are easily cut and managed by hand, removing the need to use chainsaws and trucks. Coppicing encourages us to form a relationship with, and to understand, our woodland on a practical, agricultural level. Clearing the canopy allows light to penetrate to the ground, creating a habitat for everything from butterflies to bluebells and primroses.

Like spoon carving, coppicing is itself undergoing something of a renaissance – there is a national federation here in the UK – with groups springing up all over the country, and it is to these coppicing groups that the spoon carver might be best to turn if they want a suitable bit of wood. I am keen to encourage people to care about where their piece of wood came from, to ask who owns the woodland, why a tree was felled and to learn generally about how the woodland is managed. This all helps the spoon carver join the dots on their practise.

With nearly 50 per cent of UK woodlands not actively managed, we should really celebrate any kind of woodland management as encouraging our relationship with trees. There are exceptions of course: 'clear felling', where all trees in an area are cut down, or the felling of very old trees that will take 1,000 years to grow back! But using a chainsaw doesn't necessarily equal bad practice, though I consider chainsaws to be vicious (if efficient) instruments which only

serve to distance you from the tree. 'Wood culture' certainly exists in commercial forestry – really agriculture – with its vast land management plans. It might seem counterintuitive to celebrate the use of ugly, earth-moving machinery, but if it is used as a part of what are often complex, sustainable land projects then that is surely a good thing.

But the most beautiful form of land management, perhaps, is to establish a long term plan suited to small scale management practices, and appropriate to the needs of the people working it, and to the local area. This can include fruit trees alongside growing trees for boards, all of mixed ages, as part of an 80-year plan, with scope for coppices and glades within this. For me, ideally, the coppicing would be carried out with sympathetic tools like billhooks and axes - it is empowering to be able to rely on your own skill and strength and a finely evolved tool to do the job. Using hand tools, which have evolved over the centuries we have worked in woodlands, is to have what I would call a 'good job' in wood.

As a London-based carver and seller, however, I get most of my wood from tree surgeons (who would otherwise have to pay to get rid of the dying wood I use) but I also source material from a space which is quite special to me. Tower Hamlets Cemetery Park lies in the heart of the East End of London, a seemingly-ramshackle and now disused Victorian graveyard, which is sympathetically maintained by a dedicated local charity. As well as being an important nature reserve and a fresh-air resource for the local community, it is a little overgrown, and as a result much like a woodland in the city. Crucially, it is close to where I live and work and it's a perfect place to find the green wood I need. In keeping the park safe for local residents, trees are cut down each winter, usually windblown trees or trees that are felled to create more light and a more diverse environment (we call this 'thinning') and this wood is perfect for carving spoons.

When you gain an understanding of the new wood culture, you'll realise that the materials you need will be all around you. Contact your local coppice group, a firewood merchant or a city tree surgeon. Using local resources, and knowing why and where the trees were cut will give you a new appreciation of the things you make from them.

2

The Raw Materials

Green woodwork – working with axes and knives on wood which has been freshly cut – is the work of the individual, so we can manage our own materials, without having large companies come between us and our practice.

The cost of seasoned oak, for example, is around £60 per cubic foot; a tree which has been stored by the side of a country road might retail for around £40 per ton. At this price the cost-per-spoon is so negligible that it liberates us as carvers. Any value which accumulates in commercially available wood actually comes from transporting, sawing and storing the material.

Throughout history, spoon carving has always been with green wood, and a return to green wood values is to celebrate the decision making of the craftsperson. All woodworkers must adapt to their material, as it's not homogenous, the same all the way through, like metal or clay. The green woodworker engages with it from the very first stages of the process, i.e. chopping down the tree. We must make choices how best to make use of the tree as a whole, and as a result our responsibilities as craftspeople are that much greater – certainly more so than somebody working with an already pre-processed material. Spoon makers use all of the tree, from the sturdy, interlocked fibres at the base to our prized bent branches – this last being a part that many woodworkers and timber merchants would consign to the chipper.

At this stage it may be worth saying that working with the irregularities of our material, or the dynamic qualities, is key to understanding wood culture. Another way of putting it is to say that the process of making spoons involves embracing chaos and the fact you don't have complete control over some things.

Whether you're making spoons from large rounds or branchwood, it's worth being efficient with the material if for no other reason than it increases your skills, which is always a good thing. Our basic small unit of uncarved wood – known as a 'billet' – can be cleft from the round wood in many different ways, but the general principle is to saw across the fibres of wood to set the length of the spoon and then to cleave the wood along the fibres to get the correct cross sectional size you need.

Creating a billet of the right size may well leave you with a section of wood which includes both sapwood and heartwood. Sapwood is the paler wood, full of moisture and sugar, which is found on the outer part of the branch or trunk; heartwood is the inner, mostly darker wood, which is pumped full of tannins. (Most of our woods don't have visibly distinct heartwood and sapwood.) In some varieties of wood, if we use a blank which crosses these two types then we might get an irregularly two-toned spoon.

A lot of the myths surrounding the 'flaws' of sapwood aren't really relevant in spoon carving, as it is woodwork on such a small scale. Sapwood's apparent susceptibility to fungi and its propensity to rot might be an issue if we were making a gatepost, for example, but spoons don't rot as they are never exposed to moisture for very long, and the sugars are soon washed out of them in the kitchen.

Sapwood and heartwood shrink, or dry, at slightly different rates (with woods like cherry this is exaggerated), so we may get a slightly wonky finished spoon. When wood dries it shrinks differentially – tangentially at around 10 per cent,

and radially around 5 per cent. In other words, when looking at the cross section of a log it shrinks 10 per cent along the length of the growth rings and 5 per cent across the growth rings (shrinkage along the length of a log is negligible, certainly with regards to making spoons).

If the billet has been cleft symmetrically to the grain you will get symmetrical shrinkage, and if not then it will be slightly wonkier when it dries. I try to work this into my designs to a certain extent, but it's important for a beginner not to get caught up in this stuff too much. Shrinkage might be important for the joiner or maker of larger objects to consider, but for the spoon maker the effects are negligible.

The exciting part of craftsmanship is figuring out which way the wind is blowing; with woodwork it's about discovering which way the grain is going and responding to that. The final shape of a spoon is a complex thing, the result of many fluid, accumulating processes which make up the end product. Each step taken builds upon the last, and the master craftsman takes no step rigidly. Rather, they work deftly and dynamically and respond not just to the material, but to the outcomes from the previous steps.

Sometimes you respond to the fibres of wood, which are predictable like the flow in a river. No two rivers flow in the same way, but with experience you can begin to anticipate the finer nuances of their movement over rapids, and how the flow will change at bends in the stream. The term 'organic' can be used to describe sculptural forms that are reactive and not necessarily perfectly symmetrical or uniform. Organic forms adapt and evolve according to the environmental conditions they find themselves in – by embracing this, craft is lifted beyond mere engineering. For me finding profundity in the 'organic' is the very essence

of Wabi Sabi, a Japanese concept that many westerners just interpret as finding beauty in imperfection.

This approach leads us into embracing the complexities of growing wood, and working with the idiosyncrasies of the felled tree. The grain within a branch which bears a lot of weight, for example, appears rippled where the fibres have become interlocked. This wonderful effect occurs when the tree has been loaded or under stress. As well as being beautiful – it is used in the figuring you find on the backs of violins – stressed wood also tends to be less prone to splitting, so is good for the woodworker.

Making a spoon out of a bent branch, using the natural curve in the wood as the foundation of your spoon's shape, is a really beautiful thing, and this is often the best part of a tree to use. (In part three you will find reference to several spoons that embrace the qualities of the bent branch.) For me, bent branches epitomise wood culture, and I always feel that the tree gods are going to be very happy with you for creating a spoon and embracing the material in this way. To make a spoon out of a bent branch speaks of your communion with the woodland, of sifting through piles and identifying a branch and making a conscious decision to employ that material gainfully. It is a rejoinder to our ideas of convenience and of just buying and making things out of straight planks.

The green wood spoon carver also turns other apparent 'flaws' in wood to his advantage. I sometimes work with spalted wood – which essentially means the wood is mouldy. Spalting affects the figure and pattern of the wood, which can produce a very beautiful effect, as if a pattern has been superimposed upon the grain at random. Spalting can affect the colour and sometimes gives weird, bold black lines, even zigzags; these are essentially the limits of the fungal infection within the wood. (When working with spalted wood, we almost want to make our spoon form as plain as possible to really show off the grain.)

Burrs and burls – the deformations, knots and lumps sometimes found growing on the trunks of trees – can also produce interesting patterns. They might be irritations for the tree, but the effects in the wood can be curious and beautiful for the spoon carver. Also importantly, because the fibres are more compact at these odd junctions, you don't get the usual differential shrinkage. This makes for a stronger structure if you are making a large bowled spoon, like the *Kuksa* drinking spoon (featured in chapter 6).

As an aside, I find it interesting that diseased, stressed or damaged wood can be the most sought after. This is also telling in terms of its human association: we see value in that which has undergone adversity, and away from privileged or perfect forms.

I love using plain wood best, however, because then nothing distracts from the form of the spoon. I like the egalitarian beauty which comes from a plain bit of wood. A nice clean, straight bit of sycamore is the cow parsley or stinging nettle of the wood world; this compared to the glamour of the orchid. I believe that the hunt for the rare or unique is to neglect or even despise the ordinary; when we carve a good spoon from ordinary wood we celebrate the beauty of ordinariness. This might run counter to our modern instincts - these days if I want lots of likes on Instagram, I just have to carve a few patterns on the top of a spoon, or use a highly figured piece of wood – but if you focus only on novelty or jazziness you miss the crazy beautiful normalness of fibrous forms.

I use a lot of plain sycamore and cherry, in part because they are very easy to get hold of. These materials are also good for spoons because they are close grained and strong when cut properly. If you cleave sycamore or cherry on a perfect radius and then carve it in the same plane you get a distinctive effect, with the wood displaying beautiful flecks or flames. These are the medullary rays which allow radial transport of sap. For some, this is a cheap and plain effect from a cheap and plain bit of wood, but for me it's an example of allowing the wood's inherent beauty to shine through.

This simple approach is consistent with that of spoon carvers throughout history, and the link to the artisan tradition is one I am very keen to promote. Older artisan spoons, however, don't even make use of this cleaving technique, as it takes too long and is rather fussy, and it isn't something I deliberately aim for either. However, when you have split lots of billets in a way which makes best use of the wood you end up with the grain orientated in several different ways. If I then find, when carving a particular blank, that the grain lines up on the radius, I will perhaps try to accentuate this while refining the shape, aligning the form perfectly to make the most of the medullary rays in the bowl of the spoon or on the top surface of the handle.

Fibrous woods such as cherry and sycamore/maples can be good for the pro as they can speed up work because they cut specifically along the grain. Beginners should opt for less fibrous woods such as birch, alder and lime/linden because they are more forgiving when carved. More fibrous woods dig in as soon as you are cutting up the grain, this requires more skill to control. Ring porous or open grained wood like oak and ash tend to pick up food stains and absorb liquids more readily. I'd advise beginners away from these woods as they are also very fibrous. But never say never. Close grained woods like field maple or box can be lovely as they are so creamy and dense, but they are harder to come by and rightly forest workers are less likely to cut them during thinning.

Don't be afraid of trying softer woods like birch and willow; they can be great for bent branches, as they split out more readily. Equally, tough woods like hawthorne, beech and holly are great as they are less likely to chip or split. It's also worth considering dark woods such as walnut, as they age well; paler woods, such as birch or sycamore, can become grey, so try staining with coffee or gravy browning. A proper soak in oil will prevent your spoons from soaking up food stains.

Each spoon I make is individual and it is easy enough to read them as having distinct personalities. To an extent, this will be determined by the cuts of the maker, but the buyer or user is free to read the spoon as they please. In this way spoons are the same as any sculpture. It's easy to read anthropomorphic associations into spoons, and when looking at their handles and junctions I often see hips, legs and feet. For me, the Roma spoon puffs its chest out, and the Cawl spoon is similarly proud, but has more of a moon face. Some of my other spoons have more organic associations, resembling forms from nature. So I see the octagonal handled spoon as a stem on a plant, with a fig shaped bowl.

Good spoons, then, contain evidence of humanity in the marks of the maker, but also remind us of a broader, benevolent natural world. We can achieve this sublime effect by working in harmony with the dynamic qualities of our wonderful material, and employing a mixture of skill and instinct. It is perhaps the breadth of inputs and associations which gives these small sculptural forms an unlikely power.

Part

2

Knives & Axes

3

Spoon Carving Tools

Basic Tools

The most basic woodworking tools are the knife and the axe, what we might call 'the Stone Age tool kit', although originally it would have been hard to distinguish these tools as we do now. The very first tools were likely hand axes – so cutting or pounding tools – and then at some point our ancestors shoved a handle on the end. These tools would have been used for cutting meat, leather and wood.

Although I've described them as Stone Age tools this doesn't mean that they're backward looking. There is a timeless and humane subtlety to the axe and the knife, which are the woodworking tools of the individual craftsman. Axes and knives have evolved alongside us over a huge period of human history and our bodies can hold and use them in an evolved way, which is a far cry from the back-breaking work of the factory or the discomfort of eight hours in an office chair. We're not talking about a router or a planer here, which are the woodworking tools of industrialised civilization. These industrial tools don't necessarily work less well or make a less beautiful product, but in my view they draw the individual further away from the tree, and so further away from the process.

Over the years I have used lots of different tools (when I was a child I used machinery, and gouges to hollow out spoons), but when I became a journeyman spoon carver and lived in the woods I survived with the bare minimum of kit: an axe for splitting and chopping, a knife for shaping the spoon and a bent knife for hollowing it out. Using only these fundamental tools forced me to learn the basic skills of spooncraft exceptionally well.

The Axe

I see the axe as an enduring symbol of our humanity and our roots in wood culture. Whereas the knife has a multitude of uses, you don't tend to use axes for anything other than wood. The original axe would have evolved as a tool for felling small trees, but also for shaping bits of wood.

For the spoon carver, the axe is mainly used for rough shaping a 'billet' into a spoon 'blank', a process which is described in detail in Chapter 5 of this book. But basically we use the axe to split or cleave a lump of wood into a roughly spoon-shaped unit, which we can then refine using our knife and bent spoon knife.

Although you can use an axe accurately, carving to a pencil line, to try to create the exact spoon shape with your axe is really to miss the point. The axe is by far the best tool for removing a lot of material quickly, as it carries a weight of momentum and is very efficient for this job. Conversely, to do this rough shaping with a knife, hacking away to get the desired spoon outline, would be extremely laborious.

Getting the Right Axe

The standard axe you can buy from a high street hardware store is designed for splitting fire wood or kindling and isn't really sharp enough for spoon carving. Most shopbought axes come to a rounded edge and have a convex bevel, rather than a flat bevel as we require. The bevel is the part of the tool blade which is ground away to make the cutting edge; it is the surface which actually touches the wood when we carve, guiding the edge to make the cut.

There are a few manufacturers out there who are making more appropriately ground axes for woodworking, and you will find the names of these specialists in the list of tool suppliers at the back of this book.

However, to my mind, many commercially bought tools are still not sharp enough and this, alongside the fact that no edge tool will stay sharp forever, is a very good reason to learn to maintain your own tools. At the Green Wood Guild in London, where I teach, we run an axe forging workshop where you are given a bit of rough steel and, over the course of a weekend, turn it into a beautifully functioning edge tool. This process is both satisfying and empowering, learning to shape and sharpen your own tools, as both an investment in the future of your tools and the future of your craftsmanship.

The Straight Knife

My approach to knives today is very different to when I used to travel around peddling spoons with just a bag on my back. Then I had just two knives, including a general purpose one to cut string and the like – which is actually a terrible thing to do. Cutting a string for a tarpaulin, for example, will bring the blade into contact with bits of mud on the string, meaning your knife gets blunt quite quickly. The edge of a tool is extremely precious and fragile, and when we are trying to get a razor-sharp edge, we're dealing with absolutely microscopic changes in the surface which can be affected by bits of dust and grit. Today I have learned my lesson and I'll rarely touch a bit of wood with a sharp knife if I know it's touched the floor, but rather cut the end off with an axe or saw first.

The straight knives I use today are produced in an area of Sweden famous for making knives. These days there is one large company, Morakniv, but originally there would have been many individual smiths. Mora knives are great in part because they are mass produced, and affordable, so I have 40 or so on the go, which I sharpen in batches, and use them one after the other, as they blunt. At the end of this chapter see guidance on sharpening your tools.

The bevel is the defining characteristic of an edge tool. The knives I use have flat bevels: this makes them different from your standard kitchen or pen knife, which have what some call a secondary bevel. On a straight knife this should be around 7mm in width, although this width can vary slightly along the length of the blade: the bevel should be wide enough at the hilt to guide the edge on a flat planing cut, which we use for the handle of our spoon, but also short enough at the tip to be able to make tight, concave cuts at the neck. You want your total bevel angle to be around 25 degrees, so at a fine, acute angle.

Because the straight knife has a symmetrical handle you can hold it in lots of different ways. Specific knife grips allow us to carve in different ways, and these are described in detail in the next chapter.

The Bent Knife

There are lots of different types of bent knives and many trades, not to mention many different cultures, employ them. Farriers will use them to clear horses' hooves; a wood turner will have a miniaturised version for turning his bowls, which are normally known as hooks. Some Native Americans traditionally used a *mocotaugan,* or 'crooked knife' (although in use this tool is more akin to a European drawknife).

I tend to call my bent knives 'spoon knives', as they are made in a specific style for hollowing spoons. A spoon knife

is most useful when carving the bowl of the spoon, where we use it mostly for cutting across the fibres. As with all edge tools, the bevel shape is crucial, guiding the edge into the wood and giving control. If the straight knife has a flat bevel and wants to ride on a flat bit of wood when the edge is cutting, a bent knife does the same but in a bent universe: the convex surface of our bent knife rides smoothly on the concave surface of the hollow, guiding the edge to make a clean controlled cut.

The standard bent knife has an accelerating curve, so in essence you have a tool with a range of radiuses, which is adaptable to the creation of many different types of spoons. Because of its flexibility, this is the best type of bent knife for the beginner spoon carver.

However, I like to use the bigger *twca cam* (Welsh for bent knife), which tends to have a symmetrical blade and so a single radius that takes wider shavings. To a certain extent, the use of this knife defines my personal style in spoons. Sometimes I use the *twca cam* early on in the carving process, as the perfect hemispherical hollow it creates can be used as a 'datum' – a known and predictable surface which I can then use as a reference when creating the rest of the spoon. I find that the symmetry of this knife aids accurate carving in the bowl. I can also carve across the whole diameter of the blade, giving a super smooth finish and avoiding the little furrows you can sometimes get with a small blade.

Other Tools

If you have a workshop and can invest in other kit, there are further tools that make the whole process faster, or make new things possible. In addition to being practical, some of these additional tools reaffirm our status as green wood workers. We make them out of the same materials that we use for our spoons, but perhaps from different cuts of wood. Thinking about them in relation to spoon making – sizing them for your own use, for example – will also teach you broader woodworking principles that I am very keen to promote.

The Mallet

We use the mallet for controlled splitting – so driving a wedge or axe into wood – when creating our spoon billets.

The mallet of the green woodworker is very much in keeping with our practice and not what some might imagine when you say the word 'mallet'. It is still a tool for applying a swung force, but our mallet is really quite a rough, disposable thing; we use it to hit lumps of metal very hard and the wood always loses out in the end.

You can simply make a mallet out of a lump from your pile of firewood, or an odd bit from your spoon carving stack. It's nice to make a mallet out of wood with reasonable tensile strength, so ash or hazel works well. We may also choose a piece of wood which might otherwise be impractical for our spoon work, because it has a knot in it, for example.

Choose a length which is both easy to swing – it needs to be heavy enough to give you force and momentum – and one that's a handy height to pick up off the floor. The diameter of the hitting end should be wide enough for it to stand up independently – that way you can just grab it whenever you need it. It's best to carve it down to a gradual taper, and the handle end needs only to be big enough for you to grasp comfortably.

The Wooden Wedge

I see the wooden wedge as one of the most beautiful wood-working tools. It is essentially a small lump of wood, tapered to an edge, and perhaps the simplest tool in our kit. We use it to force the fibres apart when splitting trees or logs. With just a couple of wedges and a wooden mallet you can split open a whole tree. Really whacking these wedges generates enough force and heat to give a hint of toasted wood.

A wedge is extremely quick and easy to make, and best made from a fast grown, tough wood such as beech. Using an axe and knife, split out a billet and shape it to a rectangular cross section, then taper with your axe to the desired gradient: 1:6 is pretty good. It's important that the taper has a very flat surface, though it should be rounded on the corners to prevent it falling apart when hammered. Over time, the part of the wedge that you hit will become very compressed, so bevel it heavily with the axe beforehand so that the edges don't split with repeated use – otherwise it is a balancing act. Don't make your wedge too thin or fragile or it will snap; if it is too fat it can't be driven home.

The Axe Block

An axe block is also something we can create ourselves, whose form evolves with use and comes to bear the signature of our working chops and cuts.

An axe block with mass reflects the energy that the axe throws into it, so the force all comes back into the wood. In practice, it is really just a lump of wood that we can use as a base whenever we need to use the axe (we can't just work onto the floor because if you follow through you will cause serious damage to your axe).

I believe that the hunt for

the rare or unique is to

neglect or even despise the

ordinary; when we carve a

good spoon from ordinary

wood we celebrate the

beauty of ordinariness

It doesn't really matter what sort of wood you use for your block, but be aware that if you use a softer bit of wood then obviously your axe will stick in, like a dart in a dartboard. It shouldn't wobble so needs a flat base, or better still, three legs, and it needs to be a sensible height. About 17 inches is about right for me, but you should adapt the height to allow you to lean your arm on your leg as you carve, when you are sitting down to work, for control. You ideally want your block to be around a foot or 14 inches in diameter and it can be slightly sculpted to be helpful, so angled slightly toward you, and you can add a notch or a hollow to support your spoon.

The Saw

A saw is a must in the basic kit. It is, however, a modern tool compared to the axe, knife and bent knife, and as such is not really in that same genre of tools. In spoon carving, saws are most useful for cutting across the grain, which can be laborious with an axe. In particular, they are useful for sawing logs to length in the early stages of the spoon making process.

If you already own a saw then it's likely to be a jack saw, which can be bought from any hardware store. They are long and efficient but designed to be disposable – you can't sharpen the majority of modern saws because of the way they are hardened.

The folding saw is an excellent choice for the spoon carver, as it's small and very good for getting into nooks and crannies. When folded, the handle also works as a sheath, which is very handy. I think that this is the best choice saw for the hobbyist spoon carver.

The frame saw has a wooden frame and a thin blade twisted into tension by a windlass. This tension prevents the blade from buckling in use. Many saws need thicker or wider blades to achieve the same strength, but this means more work for you to push it through the wood. The thin blade means also that you can cut curves, for example if you want to make a precise job of cutting a bent branch, or profile-shape a spoon. They are also flat packable and we like them because you can change the blade according to your task.

Adze

This adze is a fantastically efficient tool, and, like axes, use weight and momentum to chop and shave wood. However, the adze has an edge which is at 90 degrees to the plane the handle swings in. This gives you greater cutting accuracy because the edge is swung at a constant distance from the wrist, allowing very controlled micro adjustments to be made, without being knocked off track when the bevel hits the wood, as can happen with an axe.

It also has a tightly curved blade that can be used for hollowing out bowls and spoons; in the photo the adze is being used to chop through the end grain. In many ways they are a superior tool for the spoon carver, but they are not versatile like the axe, and not good for chopping down trees or splitting logs. The adze is a great tool to have in your kit but is definitely not necessary for the beginner; I made hundreds of spoons before I got one.

The Drawknife
and Shaving Horse

The drawknife is a fantastic tool, which bridges the gap between the axe and knife. It's not entirely necessary for the spoon carver, but it is a beautiful and handy tool to use, as it gives you much more power than the knife but is more accurate than the axe. The drawknife can be used in several ways but by far the best is with a clamping tool like a shaving horse. The shaving horse uses a lever that you push with your feet to very firmly clamp the wood while you work it. It is extremely quick and efficient to move and reclamp the wood; you just take your foot off the pedal. The harder you pull on the knife with your arms and body the firmer the clamp is as you push harder with your foot.

It is a lovely sensation, peeling long shavings from some clean and straight green wood, sitting on a well-made horse using a razor sharp drawknife. It just feels right, in a way that pushing sawn boards over a router table in a noisy workshop wearing respirator and ear defenders never can. And those of you who use drawknives already will know exactly what I'm talking about.

Sharpening Your Tools

If your knife becomes blunt then it is not the same tool, so learning to sharpen your knife and axe and having a simple, decent kit for doing so, is essential. You will know your knife is blunt when you have to raise the bevel to make the cut. The knife should 'bite' with the bevel rubbing – you shouldn't have to tilt the blade up to slice.

We can define sharpening here as the act of creating a shape and polishing it, all of which is done with abrasives. A cheap and effective option is to use wet and dry paper – basically a sandpaper for metal – with a very uniform particle size which leaves a nice even surface.

The key to the sharpening process is to remove metal parallel to the bevel, so moving a flat bevel with a flat action on a flat abrasive. An easy way to create a flat abrasive is to use a piece of wet and dry paper on glass; the glass should be cut to around 30mm x 80mm and have no sharp edges (you could also use a diamond or a Japanese slipstone). Place your knife a couple of centimetres inside the edge of a bench or table. Place your abrasive on top of the knife, making sure that you finger aligns with the middle of the bevel. This way you can feel if the abrasive is flat. You then move your abrasive from side to side, working along the length of the blade and bevel. When you have the cutting edge toward you, your knuckles are moving safely against the bench, away from the

blade. The best way of knowing you have sharpened right to the edge is if a 'bur' – a tiny curl of metal – forms on the tip of your blade. You can work through abrasive paper grits, rough to fine, using different types of wet and dry until you achieve a highly-polished finish.

You then give a final polish using a strop. I use a flat planed piece of hardwood on which I rub polishing compound, then drag the bevel of the knife flat along it.

The axe is sharpened in the same fashion as the knife, you need a large 9mm bevel on the inside i.e. the side that rubs the wood. When sharpening the spoon knife the emphasis should also be on the inside of the blade. Use wet and dry paper wrapped tightly around some dowel, pushing away from the edge, maintaining a flat bevel.

Sharpening a knife or axe is a bit of an art form in itself. I don't want to get too technical here, but there is more information in the online learning section of the Green Wood Guild website.

4

Knife Grips

In the next chapter we're going to make a basic spoon. However, before we start, it's a good idea to first learn and then practise the key knife grips. Some may feel strange, and seem counterintuitive to begin with, but in time they will become a part of your technique, and liberate your designs.

People who are self-taught tend to use just a couple of intuitive grips, with their initial tentative efforts (rightly) focussed on not cutting themselves, as opposed to on craft and technique. But, in the long run, using a range of considered knife grips will make for much better spoons, as different grips are more appropriate for different parts of the spoon. It will also make the experience more relaxing, as well as safer. When practised properly, they will work different muscles in your body and make the whole experience more comfortable – an important consideration if you are doing lots of carving.

These grips are definitely best practised on a softish bit of wood before you introduce them to your spoon making. I would suggest that working on some inch-thick willow wands would be a perfect way to start.

Before you try a new grip, it's best to practise the stroke without cutting any wood, so just miming the action. Then follow through very slowly to see where the knife would end up if you slipped. The first cut you actually take should be hair-thin, again to check that you are using the correct technique; the lack of force makes these first cuts much safer. Once confident that you are cutting safely and correctly, you can then move on to taking thicker cuts.

Left-handers follow the same process as right-handers but using their dominant hand, unless stated otherwise.

As discussed in the previous chapter, our knives should be extremely sharp, and obviously this carries certain risks. The activities and tools used should be treated with great care and attention. Here are some other, perhaps seemingly obvious, safety considerations, but worth mentioning:

Never carve when tired; be mindful to take regular breaks when in the zone. This can be difficult and you may have to force yourself to do this but it is perhaps the best way to prevent accidents.

Never carve when inebriated: it might sound like a nice idea to hang out, have a few beers and whittle but it isn't.

Don't wander around with razor sharp tools in your hands.

Keep tools sheathed and safely packed away when not in use.

Taking the knife out of the sheath is even worth describing. Give it a twist first, without any pulling, to loosen it. It should then be possible to remove it without resistance.

The techniques involved in spoon carving take years to master. When trying out new techniques never rush. Take your time; think what would happen if you slip or follow through. Think about where the sharp edge will end up.

As mentioned above, practise without cutting first then start gentle and small.

Being good is about skill, not strength or speed. Getting good takes time; be gentle on yourself whilst learning.

If you keep this advice in mind as you progress to learning your knife grips and carving your spoons, it'll make the whole experience safer, and more enjoyable.

The Forehand Grip

This grip is great for making long cuts along the grain, for example, when profiling the handle of your spoon. It is a good grip for removing lots of material in the early stages of your spoon production, when accuracy is less important.

How you sit when using this grip is important, however. Hold the spoon blank in your left hand, up and across your right thigh, with your hand back towards your hip. Make sure you point the handle of your spoon at the ground. Rest your wrist on the side of your thigh, supporting the spoon blank merely by stretching the tendons in your wrist, rather than pulling with any force. We then make the cut by brushing the knife down towards the floor.

Hold the knife right at the back of the 'V' or web formed between thumb and forefinger. Your thumb and forefinger then close around the knife, high up the handle, so that the belly of the knife can't slip through. Don't hold the knife too firmly with your little finger and ring finger, which can almost come off the knife completely, and let the knife angle upwards and away from the direction of travel.

Aim to use the first part of the blade, closest to the handle, literally the first centimetre. As always, practise the action without actually doing any cutting to begin with, working towards taking just a hair-thin shaving and using very little force. Consider what would happen if the knife slipped, and where it would go, before moving on to firmer cuts.

You are always aiming for the bevel to rub, and to create long shavings which leave a nice clean finish. This in turn gives you a smooth place to begin your next knife cut. If you start getting bumps where the knife is digging in, you are only giving yourself corrective work to do further down the line.

 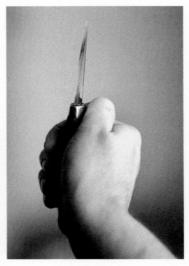

The Pull Stroke

This grip is all about having your wrist cocked, with the tip of the knife facing away from you in your hand, so, when you pull, the wrist will hit your body before the knife does. This means you can pull really quite firmly and be sure that if you follow through, you will be safe. This is great for straight or slightly concave planing cuts where you don't need huge amounts of control, like rough shaping the neck and handle.

Place the end of your blank against your chest with the end you wish to work on away from you, and simply rub the bevel of the knife on the spoon, pulling towards you to effect the cut. The force of the pull is opposed by your chest; your left hand is used to support the end of the spoon. Keep the tip of the knife vertical. This way you can be sure of where the tip of the knife is at all times, and save yourself from nicking your left hand, as may happen if you start to roll the knife horizontally.

The Reinforced Pull Stroke

This grip gives you a lot of control and can be used to great effect to refine the surface around the neck, but can also be used where accurate work is required, pretty much anywhere on the spoon.

Start with the knife edge facing towards you in your clenched fist, and bring your thumb back around the other side of the handle to rest again on your forefinger, otherwise it can get in the way. You can also brace your thumb against the back of the blade, which gives you a real feel for the bevel rubbing and increases sensitivity.

Place the spoon blank on your chest, as for the pull stroke, but now cup the hand supporting your blank around your knife hand as well. Using the two hands together like this lends you a lot of control. Keep the tip of the knife pointing at the ceiling, and angled away from you; to make the cut you only need rotate your right wrist. You must be quite careful of your left thumb, but if you keep the tip of your knife vertical and rotate the wood to adjust where you make your cuts, then it will be safely out of the way of your left thumb.

The Chest Lever Grip

This is quite counterintuitive and requires you to use your full body to work most effectively. You use your back muscles to rotate, push out and lift up your rib cage: this creates the cut. This is a very powerful grip but we don't use it for long cuts. Rather, it is perfect for cutting across the fibres, such as when we round the back of the bowl forward towards the end of the spoon, which is potentially very hard work but which can be achieved very economically with this action.

Start with your fingertips touching and palms up, knife in one palm and spoon blank in the other, with the edge of your knife facing out and away from you. When you close your knife grip into a proper fist, make certain you have your fingernails up.

Knives & Axes

This is the weird bit – but don't worry, it is meant to feel this way! Bring your hands up onto your chest with your fingernails still up. Start with the first and second knuckles of both hands on your chest and, using the first part of the blade on top of the blank, engage the edge, lock your wrists and rotate your shoulders out, pushing your ribcage up through the action. Your forearms, hands and wrists act together as two levers, with your chest as a fulcrum; your knuckles should not leave your chest. The action of your hands should mirror one another and in this way the action is similar to scissoring. With practice, because this is such a powerful grip, you can work with the full length of the knife, to carve right across the spoon.

Knife Grips

The Wrist Push

Here you push with the heel of the palm of your knife hand, which is where the force should come from. Your fingers are there only to stop you from dropping the knife. This grip is very good for cutting straight lines because the blank is supported along its length.

Place your blank on the leg of your dominant side, supporting it along its whole length – this allows us to apply consistent force along the entirety of the cut. Work with the tip of the knife ever so slightly raised to protect yourself. For safety, push with your whole body and not just your arm, and slide your forearm alongside your leg as you make the cut.

The Thumb Pull

I often use this grip for putting a chamfer on the end of a
spoon, which gives a neat, rounded-off end to the handle.
But really it is good for many other parts of the spoon carving process – for example, making a controlled cut around
the rim of your spoon.

Start with your palm horizontal and the knife handle in
line with your second knuckles, and the sharp edge running vertically; close your fingers high around the handle.
Your palm is still open and so you effect the cut simply
by the action of closing your grip. When you close the
grip you want your forefinger to be around the back of
the blade, with the fingertip coming back down onto the
handle, which gives you maximum leverage. It is best to
look straight at your hand, with the tip of the knife pointing
at the ceiling, and as you are pulling against your thumb
it is important to have this offset, sticking out at about 10
o'clock (for lefties this is two o'clock), so there's no chance
of cutting it off.

Pondering the possibilities of subtly combined function and effortless archaic beauty is the obsession of the spoon carver

The Shin Grip

This cut is ideal if you are looking to make powerful cuts along the grain, such as taking bulk off the back of the handle. The knife stays completely solid, locked against your lower leg between shin and knee, and we effect the cut by moving the spoon blank. Aim to get the wood cutting directly in line with where your knife is supported.

When I am making this cut I literally place the back of the blade against my knee or shin and then draw the wood back towards me. The shaving is coming from the part of the blade which is most supported, rather than the tip where I am not getting any leverage.

It is important to approach your cuts with the edge of the knife at an angle. Drawing the blank diagonally across the blade like this is always good practice and very much aids the efficiency of our cuts. This allows you to employ a longer length of blade and bevel; it also bites more readily and cuts a flatter surface. By way of an analogy, the best way to walk up a steep slope is by zigzagging, so lessening the gradient.

The Thumb Push

This grip is great for short, sharp cuts and is particularly useful for smoothing things down and making final adjustments, such as on the back of the bowl and the tight curves of the neck.

The emphasis here is on the position of your left thumb. Position your left hand in such a way that your thumb could rub directly where you want to make your cut. You can then place your left thumb against the back of your knife. You simply use the extension and stretch of your thumb to 'push' the cut, using the part of the blade that is slightly offset to where your thumb is. Your right hand is only really there to support the knife.

The Thumb Pivot

This is useful for getting into nooks and crannies because it gives you a lot of control, and you get a longer cut than with the thumb push. Turn the thumb push into a thumb pivot by having your left thumb even more offset to create a pivot point. However, this time you use your right wrist: twist it to rotate the blade about the thumb pivot.

For more power and control (useful for cutting across the grain at the neck) move the pivot point closer to the tip of the knife. If you do this, the handle moves a lot but the blade tip hardly at all, giving a lot of leverage and a controlled cut.

5

How to Carve a Basic Spoon

Armed with your tools and your knife grips, this chapter will now guide you through the simple method of creating a spoon. The expert will of course have his own preferred ways, mixing intuitively what I have here broken down into discreet stages; over time you too will learn to follow your instincts in the way that you address the wood and create your spoon. But the skills you will learn here in creating a bowl, neck and handle will give you a good grounding in the fundamentals of making, and lend themselves to a huge variety of spoons, including the sixteen found in part three of the book.

There are shortcuts you could employ. You might be tempted to cut out the profile of your spoon with a bandsaw, for example, but this would be to distract you from the real joy of sculpture, which to me is working in three dimensions rather than two. In using an axe you are thinking in three dimensions from the outset, a method that gives you a real feel for the material, with each cut exploring the properties of the wood. This all adds to your understanding of wood's strengths and weaknesses, and ultimately informs how you design your spoon.

Creating the Billet

The very first thing we have to do is create the billet. This is the basic unit of wood, cleft with an axe or froe, from which we create our spoon. The green wood that we use is wet and therefore easy to split, or cleave, along the fibres. Seasoned wood won't cleave so readily, so modern woodworkers who can never be sure of the grain direction in a sample tend to rely on using bandsaws and abrasives to shape to their work.

We cleave the wood, as leaving it 'in the round' makes a weak spoon prone to splitting, because wood doesn't shrink evenly as it dries. When left in the round, it effectively pulls itself apart. After splitting the wood we should still remove the pith (the very centre of the branch or log) and the first two or three inner growth rings. This is immature growth and the tight radius of the rings make it particularly prone to splits.

There are two ways of cleaving the wood along the grain: radially, which produces wedge shapes, much like cutting a birthday cake into slices, or tangentially, which is in essence splitting parallel to the growth rings. Woods like cherry have a distinctive heartwood, so splitting the wood radially gives you a lovely two tone billet containing both heartwood and sapwood. Wood that has been split perfectly tangentially will give you a series of circles in the bowl of the spoon. As you hollow deeper into the bowl, you work your way through successive growth rings, creating an effect similar to contour lines on a map. This is desirable if we are aiming for precise effects, as with the feather spoon. However, in most cases I don't tend to overthink potential patterns and arrangements.

To cleave wood, we use an axe and a wooden mallet. Simply place the wood on the far side of your axe block, rest the edge of the axe where you would like to make the split and hit the axe on the top with the mallet. For control and safety, it is good to start with small taps and then build up to firmer ones if they are needed. The axe tends to simply penetrate the wood at first, before it starts sending a large split down the length of the fibres; when you feel it begin to split you can gently tap it apart.

You really don't need to whack the axe as this could send the wood flying away from you (at which point you'll just have to go and pick it up). We also don't want the razor-sharp axe dislodging and swinging out like a pendulum. For extra safety it is important to hold the axe at 90 degrees to your body, so that if the axe does dislodge, it pendulums away from you. Always double up on safety practices: make sure that you are performing your technique correctly in the first place, but also have a failsafe procedure, so even if you do make a mistake then you are still protected.

If your axe gets stuck, never try to pull it out with one hand on the axe and the other clutching your piece of wood. This can cause accidents. If possible, pick the axe up with two hands, with the log still attached, and continue tapping down on the far side of your axe block until the log is split. Alternatively, you could use a wooden wedge to force the fibres apart.

Most of my spoons are made from logs between six and twelve inches in diameter, though any size is fine as long as you can create a billet big enough for the spoon you'd like to make. The smallest bit of wood we can realistically use is a branch cleft in half. As a beginner, it's a good idea to start with a billet the size of a cooking spoon – so about 11 inches long and 2½ inches wide and ¾ inch thick. The billet is then sawn to approximately the same length as the spoon we wish to create, plus an extra quarter of an inch or so.

Truing up the Billet

Beginner spoon carvers often end up with very wonky spoons because they start with an asymmetric billet, so it's important to start with a 'true' billet. A radially cleft piece of wood presents you with a triangular billet, and to true this up we simply take away some of the material from one side to create a more rectangular shape. You may also have some bark to remove at this stage.

Creating the Blank

The start of the spoon carving process involves turning your billet into what we call a 'blank', something which roughly resembles a spoon. Creating a blank as described below is the gateway to creating most of the spoons in this book, and requires us to use an axe.

Creating the Cross Section of the Spoon

When using an axe as you will here, 'choke up' the handle with your hand close to your head. It is essential that you tuck your fingers away on the hand holding the spoon blank. Make sure you think through each cut before lifting the axe; there should be no mindless action.

For all axe work on your block, you should always be able to simultaneously see both your spoon-holding hand and the axe all the way through its swing, so the bit of wood you are working on is leaning back towards you. When working higher up the blank, make sure you never lift the axe high enough to be able to come back down onto your spoon-holding hand. These delicate cuts are made with just a flick of the fingers and wrist, no arm movements.

The first phase of creating our blank is to develop the cross section, or 'end on' view of the spoon bowl. We do this by removing material from the underside of our spoon, from about halfway, using the axe to shave the wood away. This creates three broad facets – the name given to the surface created by any edge tool on the wood – which run all the way down the billet. These original facets are very important and dictate the depth and shape of the bowl of the spoon going forward. It's important to leave wide, square edges at this stage, as this gives us options later in the design process. Also, to remove too much wood from the edge at this stage is to potentially compromise the form of the bowl. Always try to think in three dimensions, as a change in shape in one dimension often has consequences that affect the other two.

When creating a spoon you always begin with straight lines, no matter how elegant and ergonomic you may desire your finished spoon to be. Carving is a process with steps to it and our final, complex shapes are created via defined, linear steps.

We can begin to chop away the sides of the handle, using the axe to cut across the fibres. To remove a lot of bulk from the blank we employ a chopping action where the axe makes chips. When chopping, gently tilt the blank so that the axe edge cuts the wood around 60 degrees: at this angle the axe penetrates the wood really well, easily separating it out along the fibres – this creates our chips. (I find this part of the process beautiful and the mere act of chopping teaches you a lot about the material.) With the blank now held more vertically you can then clear the chips with a shaving action, allowing the bevel of the axe to rub and shave the chips away.

Next, I would add a crank to my spoon. The crank is the change in the shape of the spoon in side profile – the curve which allows us to dip a spoon into a bowl without putting our fingers into the food too – and which holds our hand in a helpful position in relation to the bowl of the spoon. For me, a crank is ultimately essential to the form of a great spoon, lending an extra dimension to the design and transforming the spoon into a kind of sculpture. However, if this is your very first spoon you may wish to skip this step. You should really make a straight spoon first as adding a crank requires a more complex axe technique.

Before you make the axe cuts which will define the angle of the crank coming into the bowl, you first need to break the fibres in the bowl with the lower point or heel of your axe. We do this because the wood naturally wants to split along the fibres, and if you come in at a steep angle, as we need to when adding crank, you may end up splitting the whole top off your bowl. Severing the fibres with the point of the axe releases the natural tension in the wood fibres. You are going to hollow out the bowl later so it doesn't matter if you employ quite rough cuts at this stage.

Lean the spoon blank into your axe block, with the handle towards you at less than 45 degrees. Then use your axe to slice across the fibres, chopping down the handle into the first part of the bowl of the spoon (into what we might call the shoulder of the bowl), with the aim of creating the angle we want for our crank. When you have removed this material, you can flip the spoon around and work back with a similar slicing action, back toward the centre of the bowl, using the edge of the block to stop the axe.

Rounding the Back or the Underside of the Bowl Forward

The best way to round the back of your spoon forward is to employ the bump cut. Place the axe on the back of your blank, just past the halfway point of what will be your bowl, where you intend to make the deepest part. Starting with the blade on the wood like this gives you more control. Tilt the axe until the edge bites, then carefully lift the axe and blank together and 'bump' them down onto your block.

Between each cut drop the spoon handle slightly to gently alter the angle at which the axe goes into the spoon and begin to create the curving underside, taking it forward towards the rim. By adding two 'bumped' facets more at than 45 degrees to the original, you should get a dome shaped bowl. I would recommend leaving thickish, square edges (around 4mm) because this gives you more options in shaping the rim, but I'm happy to create a sharper edge towards the very corners of the blank.

If the handle is still really fat you can now do some more chops with the axe. You may also need to take some bulk off the back of the bowl (but be aware that you will be using the axe quite close to your fingers).

Creating the Finished Spoon

We have now created our basic spoon blank, and can begin creating a finished spoon. Take your straight knife and begin to 'dress' the surface of the top of the bowl of the spoon. This is perhaps the hardest surface to get right, so we need to do this first and work all the other surfaces up accordingly.

This process requires a variety of knife grips. You can use the reinforced pull stroke for the majority of the bowl, from the very tip back down towards the neck of the spoon.

You can then come back down into the bowl using the thumb push, and start to shape the rim by going across it using the thumb pull.

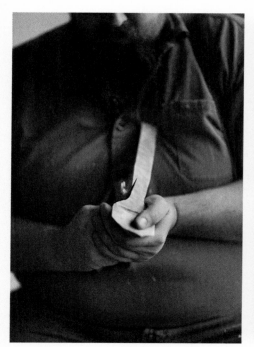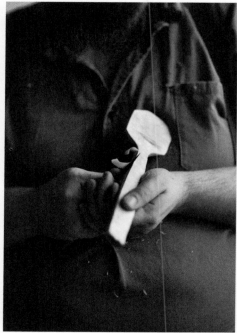

Now you can begin to make the neck symmetrical. I tend to work by sight but you may find it helpful to mark out three central points along the length of your spoon with a pencil. Start with a centre mark at the very end of the handle, and one at the neck, then 'sight down' these two and line up a third point at the very end of the bowl. You will then have a good visual guide with which to work. Making sure your carving centres on these three points will take you a very long way to controlling the finished form.

 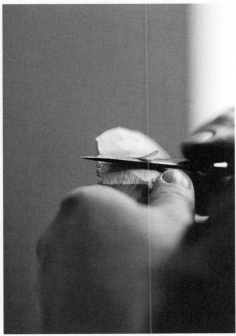

Begin to shape the back of the bowl by using the chest lever grip, refining it from about halfway towards the front of the bowl. This part should always be convex, as to create a flat or concave surface here will mean a weak structure prone to splitting. Be sure to leave a thin square edge of around 2 or 3mm and be careful not to come too far back towards the neck, as this will mean carving 'up the grain'. If you do this the knife could dig into the fibres and possibly split off the side of the bowl.

You can now use the reinforced pull stroke to carve back towards the neck, shaping the second half of the back of the bowl. Try to leave some depth to the neck where it is thinnest (as seen from above) to retain strength. Getting a smooth finish in the tight curves of the neck can be quite tricky, so it may be best to refine this area using the thumb pivot grip.

When creating our rim, we are aiming to achieve three things: an even, square rim of 2 to 3mm thickness; a nice rounded dome shape to the back of the bowl; and a symmetrical profile. Focus on creating a square rim by using the thumb pull when profile shaping the rim, and the thumb push on the back of the spoon. The rim is a delicate part of the spoon and should be smooth and refined.

Now we begin the organic, or intuitive, process of refining the neck and handle. We are working towards having a fairly triangular cross section at the neck that flattens to a gentle U-shape at the end of the handle, which gives us even strength along the length of the spoon. You could also add a chamfer to the end of your spoon using the thumb pull.

Hollowing the bowl is the last part of the basic spoon carving process and here we employ our bent knife. Before you begin, mark the boundary of the rim of your spoon on the top surface of the blank with a pencil line, running your finger around the rim and etching in a line 2 or 3mm wide.

Using the axe block to support the spoon, hold your bent knife at the blade end of the handle and brace it with your thumb (if the handle length allows) with your elbow resting on your leg. Starting on the side closest to you, cut across the fibres of the bowl with your bent knife. Rotate your wrist to give control and a nice curved action. Begin with a small cut and work towards the axe block, taking gradually longer shavings. You will create a shallow hollow and slowly get deeper into the spoon, working your way outwards, left and right. (Shown opposite, highlighted in blue.)

The vast amount of hollowing is done across the grain in this way. To tidy up the rim, use the following knife grips. It's important that you work from the top of the bowl down towards the sides, and from the handle end of the bowl up towards the sides. Using these grips we are able to work the four quarters of the bowl whilst always carving down or across the grain.

Employ the thumb pull grip. Be extra careful to make sure all of your thumb is on the back of the spoon, in case you follow through. It can be difficult to keep your thumb in position so rest it on your leg to keep it steady.

You can also use the bent knife with the reinforced pull stroke, using the long handle to give you more control. For one corner of the bowl, work with your spoon handle resting against your chest, for the other have the spoon facing away from you and resting on your leg. Slipping does happen occasionally so keep your thumb tucked away.

Finally, using the reinforced pull stroke again, with your

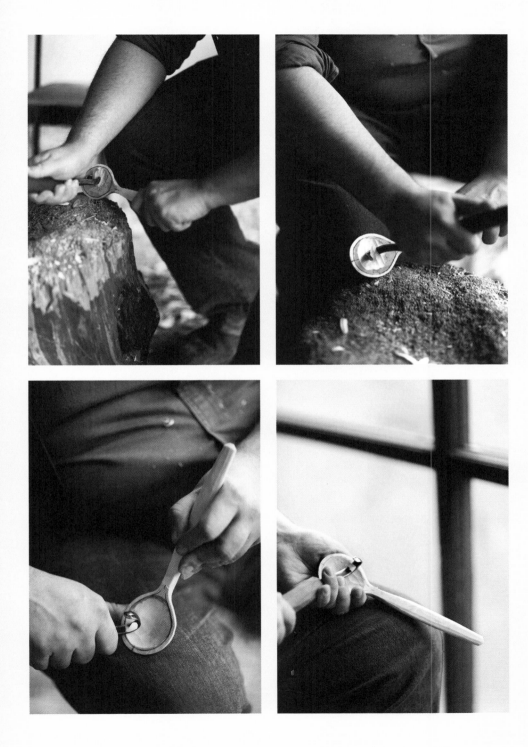

spoon-holding hand on your leg and spoon handle on your knee, use your fingers as a pivot point and slowly rotate the knife around the back corner of the bowl. In a similar way you can hold the spoon bowl and pivot using your fingers, this time rotating the spoon around the knife, a bit like an ice cream scoop. It's important to stop in the centre of the spoon to avoid following through and cutting your hand.

To work the opposite side of the bowl and avoid working too close to your palm, flip the whole spoon around and continue with the same grip. This grip is great for getting to the bottom of the bowl.

Maintain thickness in the centre of the bowl and fineness at the rim as far as you possibly can: if the rim is too fine it will chip easily; too fat and it won't move through your food smoothly. (An eating spoon obviously needs to be much more refined than a cooking spoon.) The decisions you make will always be compromises between strength, function and style.

For more guidance on hollowing the bowl and all basic spoon carving techniques, see the videos and resources on my website.

Finishes

The carved facets from a razor-sharp knife are clean and smooth, and go a long way to giving our spoons a good finish. This is so much nicer than a roughly sanded spoon whose grain furs up as soon as it gets wet in use.

Spoons tend to age well as long as they have all of their sharp edges removed. If cared for reasonably well, they are hardy kitchen companions. It is, however, best not to pop them into a dishwasher. After washing, it's also nice to give your spoons a chance to dry gently, rather than putting them on a radiator or leaving them to fester in a damp utensil holder!

A spoon will pick up stains from food and gain a patina – a nice word for dirt – from our hands; a white spoon will often end up with a brown bowl and a slightly grey handle. This actually looks much nicer than it sounds! Of course, different woods also age differently, but, on the whole, they all look nicer for the ageing process. In my shop, people often express worry about staining their spoons with food, but, ironically, if I ever have an old spoon lying around, it is always the first that people want to buy!

It is not always necessary to add a finish to spoons, and mostly I don't. This is partly out of laziness and partly as swelled oil can take some of the character of the cuts away. That said, I am not totally opposed to oiling spoons, which works better than waxing (wax tends to run out of the spoon when it gets warm).

Oiling is particularly appropriate with steeper sided bowls, which tend to have shorter grain more prone to splitting as the spoon gets wet and dries out repeatedly. Oils that harden in the wood are good because they set and don't run out of the grain in use. The classic natural oils which set are walnut, linseed and tung oil. It is important to make sure that the oil you buy is food-safe; a good way is to use an oil which is sold as food. If you gently warm the oil before applying it to your spoon then it penetrates deeper. Be aware that these natural oils can take a while to set. It's best if you coat your spoon generously, letting it soak in for a hour before wiping off the excess. Then leave it for a week or so to dry. Anytime you are heading away on holiday is a good opportunity to re-oil your spoons.

Within the spoon carving fraternity, the question of finishing spoons can be a contentious one, but as ever it's best to listen to advice, try it out and then see what works for you.

When I make a spoon I
am also chasing a feeling,
or rather to be able to
communicate or prompt an
emotion in a person when
they pick it up.

Part

3

The Spoons

6

Measuring Spoons

Caddy
Spoon

Feather
Spoon

Kuksa

Flour
Scoop

A measuring spoon is a supremely useful thing in the modern kitchen, despite the ubiquity of scales and other measures. A measuring spoon means you don't have to faff around with bulky instruments, and, whether fumbling with your porridge while half-awake, or adding a teaspoon of something to your baking at the last minute, the convenience of a specific measuring spoon makes life easier.

I very much enjoy the alchemy of recipes, and measuring is a key part of that, as much as managing cooking temperatures and timings, and the mechanics of stirring. Measures are part of the language of cooking and there is something magical about how, if you are making something for the first time, a dish suddenly begins to take shape out of a disparate collection of seemingly unrelated ingredients. You put faith in your recipe, and an accurate spoon measure is a tool that guides you on your journey. The whole experience is transformative. By following the same recipe and using the same measures as have been written down through the ages, you are following in the footsteps of past cultures (or perhaps your nan).

Caddy Spoon
(or Tablespoon Measure)

Caddy spoons are designed to fit inside a caddy, which is simply a container for holding dry goods like flour or sugar. Apart from the specific size of the bowl here, which is made to our tablespoon measure, the defining feature of this spoon is the short handle which allows you to leave it in the container. In an ideal pantry you might have a range of caddies containing many different dry goods, and leave a spoon in each one.

Traditionally, I suppose, we might think of a 'tea caddy', though the tablespoon-size measure we create here is really too big for tea. This scoop is perhaps best used as a coffee measure, for making coffee in a cafetière.

The distinct whale shape you end up with is certainly part of the design and of a similar style to the Swedish eating spoon in chapter 9, but this is a much stockier version. The thumb tab, resembling a flicked tail, is definitely inspired by the whale and it has a nice triangular cross section which allows your fingers to fit comfortably on the back; the top meanwhile is slightly concave so it feels nicer on the thumb. I also like the way the rib runs all the way down the back of the spoon.

When creating this spoon, it is important to start with

the right size and shape of wood. This spoon is obviously quite deep so there is going to be a lot of end grain to cut across, and cutting end grain is hard work. It is helpful to start with a fairly long and thin billet, which isn't too far away from your desired cross section. Personally, I would cleave the wood down to around 40 by 60mm then shave it on a horse to a fairly square cross section. If you don't have a shaving horse then the wrist push or shin grip are good for long controlled cuts on straight wood like this.

You can make a few of these spoons at one time out of a long blank – carve one down and cut it off before beginning the next. However, if you are making only one spoon it's still good to start with a longish length of wood. This is useful when holding the wood in a vice or horse, but it also makes the blank generally easier to handle. Put the crank into the top of the spoon using a spoon knife to cut directly across the fibres, instead of an axe. This spoon has some tight curves in the neck and the back of the tail which is a perfect place to practise the thumb pivot grip using your index finger for control.

To have a very accurate measure, you need a flat-topped spoon, which means an aesthetic compromise, because these spoons look best with a slightly concave top surface. I'm happy to use a concave design, as a heaped tablespoon is also a practical measure. If, however, you require a very accurate measure then you can style your bowl accordingly.

Measures are slightly different in different countries – for example, in the UK a tablespoon is 17.5ml but in Australia it is 20ml. So we start with a bought tablespoon and create our measure from that. First place a layer of clingfilm in the bowl of the spoon before moulding some plasticine into the standard measure, and then measure it off. You can then decide what shape of bowl you want to make and mould your plasticine accordingly, knowing that it will give you the right capacity. This shape is now our guide.

I use a small *twca cam* – the bent knife with a perfect radius – to get the same size cut over and over again, but the hollow can be achieved with a standard spoon knife too.

Another thing you need to factor in at this stage is that your bowl is going to shrink, so we need to cut a bowl which is slightly larger than the measure we finally need. Knowing by how much will come with experience, but aiming for the rim to be 3 or 4mm higher than necessary should give you enough leeway for shrinkage. Leave the spoon to shrink for a couple of weeks or, alternatively, you can put it into the oven overnight at around 90 degrees Celsius (195 degrees Fahrenheit, Gas Mark ¼). Once the spoon has dried and shrunk you can reinsert the plasticine (the cling film keeps the wood clean) and carve down the rim of the bowl to the correct level.

Feather Spoon
(or Teaspoon Measure)

This beautiful spoon creates the sense of a feather through the correct choice of wood, alignment of the wood's grain within the blank, and careful carving.

The chevrons running down the handle are created by cutting through the growth rings – more growth rings equals more chevrons. To make the feather spoon we use slowly grown wood. This means that each year the tree puts on a small amount of growth which in turn means more rings per inch and more chevrons. Slow grown wood is not hugely strong but fine for a small spoon like this. We tend to use a measuring spoon quite gently and as such it isn't really subject to the stresses of cooking or eating, like being dipped in boiling water, or used to rub and scrape.

When held in your hand you can feel that the spoon has a pronounced rib or 'quill' along the top of the handle, which in part creates the feather effect. There is a general curve upwards of the handle which gives a sense of crank, which is important because it allows you to put the bowl of the spoon fully into whatever you're spooning without dipping your fingers in too.

I've used elm here, which is what we call 'ring porous', meaning that you get distinct grain pattern, alternating between dense summer growth and porous spring growth. We need to start with a fairly big blank, giving us enough depth to cut down the grain on the handle. The billet needs to be perfectly tangentially split, as carving down through the layers symmetrically gives us the feather effect and also creates these lovely circles in the bowl.

Create the feathering of your handle first by carving broad facets down it with your knife, centring the chevrons. It is best to get this done early on, before you start to remove the bulk off the back of the blank. If you start at the end of the handle near the bark of the blank then you can also get the sapwood-heartwood contrast, which adds even more to our design. After this, use your bent knife to carve down towards the centre of the bowl, heading down through the growth rings, with each layer creating a stripe.

We create our accurate teaspoon measure in much the same way as we do the tablespoon, by using clingfilm and plasticine.

Kuksa
(or Measuring Cup)

This is really a dual purpose spoon, equally useful as a measure in the kitchen or as a cup for drinking. The crank of the handle means it is great for dipping, whether into a sack of flour or a bucket of water. If you are the outdoors type you may find it useful for collecting water from a stream. My design is based upon the Scandinavian-style *Kuksa*, and I think there is no finer way to drink coffee than from a *Kuksa*.

Swedish culture has this idea of 'Fika' which very much chimes in with my own ideas about society, food and work. I have taught at spoon carving workshops in Sweden, and if somebody mentions coffee, then joyous chirps of 'Fika!' chorus around. Fika isn't taken at strict times like our 'elevenses' or afternoon tea, but usually involves chatting and cake of some kind too. It seems that the emphasis is on the positive, social aspect of coffee and cake, rather than the less joyous 'tea break' concept we have here in the UK, which still defines your time in terms of work, even if it is a break from it.

This links in to the Danish lifestyle concept of *hygge* – a gentle and cosy activity that is soft on the senses, heart-warming and rewarding. Eating, cooking and crafting communally is a big part of how, as social animals, our culture has evolved. So it is no surprise that in wood cultures such as Scandinavia it is traditional to sit and carve together, and particularly to carve a beautiful functional spoon for a loved one.

The walls of the bowl of this spoon will have what we call a short grain, comprised of short fibres, which are very prone to splitting because they will absorb water very easily. This can force the shape of the spoon to change as it swells with water, and then shrinks as it dries.

To counter this, you could also use a burl, which effectively gives you a net of fibres, or a burr, where hundreds of little knots have formed in the wood. Both would provide greater strength, but I think a burl is better as it's almost as if you were using a bent branch, but with the fibres bending in all directions rather than just one. This means that when our drinking spoon gets wet in use, even though the fibres swell in many directions, the spoon is not weak at any particular point. However, these can be difficult to find, so I normally use a bit of wood from the base of a tree. Here the wood is stronger as the base has been toughened by many years of swaying and storms. The forces of movement have been concentrated in this part of the tree and the grain reacts by becoming interlocked.

The design allows you to add bulk to the weakest points – and to a certain extent this happens naturally in the manufacturing as cutting across the grain is hardest so people tend to leave more bulk on the ends. The thumb tab end which forms the handle also adds strength to the weak end-grain wall, and the other end has a keel like a boat. Some people accentuate these functional features into bird-like forms with the keel at the front turned into beak/head shape and the handle as tail feathers. This can be done very subtly or as given an almost lifelike quality, using paint.

Often with this style of spoon, it is more convenient to hollow the bowl first as you can clamp it by the sawn square ends, whereas if you shape the outside first it is much harder to clamp. Carving this deep bowl is a lot of effort, so start with an adze if you have one to remove much of the bulk. If you are able to clamp the wood using a vice, shaving horse or folding wedges on a bench you will be able to use your spoon knife two-handed to create more force.

Another technique that is worth exploring for the experienced spooner is a neck strap. Using a long handled *twca cam*, a strap is fixed to the shaft of the blade as a pivot point, then looped over your neck. Your neck then becomes like a third arm, adding strength and manoeuvring the pivot point of the *twca* as well as freeing up your spare hand to hold the *Kuksa*. This technique is also fantastic for small bowls and large ladles.

When creating our rim, we want it to be able to pour nicely. Rims which curve out, or overflow, don't work so well and quite a steep rim with a sharp edge is best – though of course the rim should be smooth where your lip rests.

If you are aiming for an accurate cup measure you could weigh out (or use a measuring jug to measure) 250ml of flour, and this will give you a guide. Once the *Kuksa* is dry enough, the flour can then be placed inside and then the rim carved down to the correct level.

Flour Scoop

This spoon is particularly suited to sticking straight into container or stack of dry goods, and, the cylindrical shape makes it ideal for filling bags with small openings, but you can really adjust the spoon's size depending on your purpose. This is a durable spoon. It works very well as a flour scoop, but thinking of it as a vessel for moving corn, or boiled sweets, gives you a good sense of the strength we need at the rim and handle. A lot of people use this type of spoon to distribute feed for their ducks or chickens, dispersing the grain over a wide area quickly and efficiently. Spoons for outdoors use are particularly good in wood, because in winter metal spoons are deeply uncomfortable in the hand. Whatever size we want, we make this spoon out of straight-grained wood as this means the rim has strength which it needs when forcefully pushed into the material to be moved.

Start by making your billet into a rough cylinder using your axe or shaving horse. Begin by making the billet square first, then octagonal, and then take the corners off. You are looking to create nice symmetrical, parallel facets running down the blank as this makes an even cylinder. Axe out the handle of the scoop before you begin the hollowing. Chop

down the handle with the axe and thin down the cylinder until you have your handle shape. The handle needs to fit comfortably in your hand but wants to be quite thick, almost bulbous. It should line up approximately with the middle of the back of the bowl, so the shovelling action puts force directly in line with the rim that is being pushed into the material.

Then we can begin hollowing. For a large scoop an adze will save a lot of time but a small scoop can be made quickly with a spoonknife. The hollow could also be made using a drill going straight into the end grain or by turning the scoop on a lathe. This works particularly well as the handle can be turned too. For this scoop I use an adze. Starting at the rim end of the hollow, I use a chopping action to release big chips right at the end of the scoop, and then work in the same place for several chops until there is a sizeable indent into the form. Still chopping in the same direction, you can now work bit by bit back towards the handle end whilst still sending chips out the front of the scoop. Once the adze is in, it guides itself easily, as you are working with the grain.

Complete the hollow using a spoon knife; you would ideally clamp the scoop so you can use two hands on the knife. You could also work holding the scoop in one hand and supporting the end of the scoop on a block. Do this in a way so that the if the spoon knife should slip it would fly into the block rather than your hand.

The surface from the adze may be rough and need tidying up with cuts across the grain first. Once it's smooth enough you can cut along the grain at the end of the scoop, as this is more efficient and leaves a smoother finish. The walls need to be no less than 3mm thick. The rim needs a certain amount of thickness for strength, but you also want a degree of bevelling on the rim so that it cuts more readily into the dry material and also protects the rim from splitting out along the grain, which a fat square rim may be prone to. You can check the uniformity and finish of the scoop by putting your thumb and forefinger either side of the wall, and running it around to create a 3D mental picture of the surfaces by feel alone. This is a surprisingly accurate measure and one worth using when making the majority of our spoons.

7

Cooking Spoons

Standard
Cooking
Spoon

Bent
Branch
Shovel

Roma
Spoon

Turned
Spoon

Cooking spoons are probably the type of spoons which people are most used to seeing in wood. They come into their own whether you are scraping tomatoes out of a tin into a pan, trying to flip a bit of bacon, smearing flour in a béchamel sauce, stirring a risotto – even tasting a sauce from the pan. People obviously cook in many different ways, employing very many basic yet fundamental techniques, and all of these need to be reflected in the cooking spoon. I wouldn't describe myself as a 'foodie' necessarily, but, as a spoon carver, I end up thinking a lot about what you might call the mechanics of cooking.

The very biggest cooking spoons I make are for when you have a hundred people to cater for and the result is a spoon more akin to a canoe paddle! But the spoons in this chapter are really just tools for your cooking, and their dimensions should only ever reflect the size of the pans and other implements you are using.

Behind all of this, however, there is an implicit recognition that cooking is good – but that sharing food, cooking for others and especially serving them, is a really fine thing to do.

Behind all of this, however, there is an implicit recognition that cooking is good – but that sharing food, cooking for others and especially serving them, is a really fine thing to do.

Standard
Cooking Spoon

Here we create what we might call a leaf shape. This is not shovel-ended, as we will see in other cooking spoons, as this shape would be quite weak in the straight wood we use here. Rather, this spoon has a large, flat area and a definite point which allows you to get right into the corner of a pan, and to accommodate both these things we make the standard cooking spoon asymmetrically.

I tend to make a cooking spoon anywhere between 8 and 18 inches in length. For everyday use, however, you don't want it to be bigger than strictly necessary because it will overbalance in the pan. You really want to be able to leave your spoon in there. In an ideal kitchen, therefore, you would have a few different sizes, depending on your pans and the purposes of your spoons. A good all-rounder tends to be around 11 inches.

The style of this spoon is very similar to our standard eating spoon – covered in chapter 9 – and the production method is much the same. However, the cooking spoon design has a much blunter and thicker rim than the eating spoon to protect it from chipping and wearing away in the pan. It is a modern-shaped spoon, for modern-shaped pans with sheer sides that come to sharp corners where they

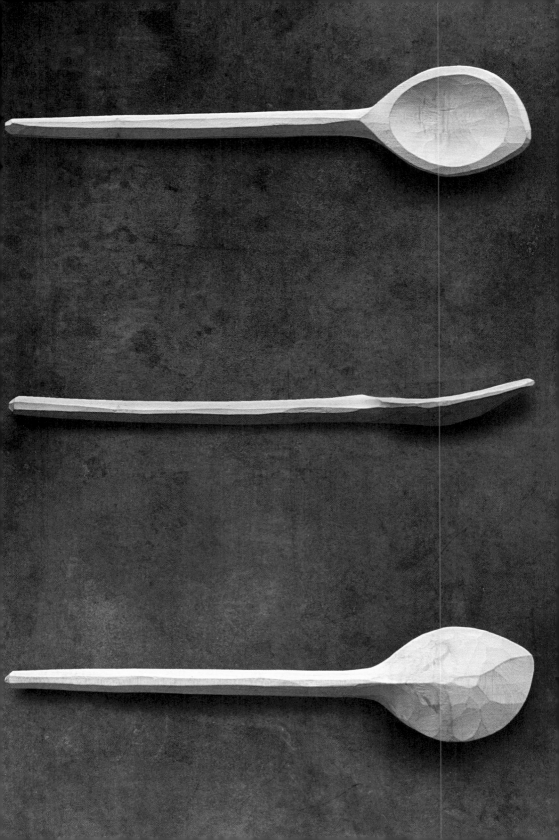

intersect with the base. My guess is the rounder designs of many historical cooking spoons were made to fit well in rounder, older-style cooking pots.

Even when aiming to create a smooth, flowing shape it is easiest to start with straight lines first. This may ultimately be an asymmetric spoon, but make the bowl with symmetrical straight cuts at the neck and the sides. Then cut the front of the bowl with a diagonal line rather than a square one. Once you have created straight lines you can then begin to smooth the surfaces down into each other to create the 'leaf' curves.

Proportionally, this spoon has a long handle, tapering all the way down to the tip. The tapering I think looks elegant and also stops the spoon from overbalancing, but that is not to say you couldn't try a similar design with a flaring handle, or a wider and flatter handle. Either way, it is important that the end of the handle is rounded as you are often using it end on, and you want it to be comfortable in your hand.

Because this spoon is made out of straight-grained wood, and because we will use this spoon for scraping, we need to think a little about the strength of the rim. We don't take the spoon to a sharp, narrow edge at the rim because this would wear or chip easily. If anything, the rim is widened, so it takes longer to wear down. You should leave a long patch on the top of the rim which runs straight with the fibres, then create a crisp, bevelled edge all the way around.

Bent Branch Shovel

Making a spoon from a bent branch is a true sign of wood culture. Such spoons tend to be made for loved ones rather than by artisans knocking them out by the hundred as they require more time and obviously specialist material, a material that these days is usually discarded as wood chip! This spoon is also the pragmatist's choice: it is a much better spoon because it utilises the natural bend in the wood to create a bowl shape where the wood fibres run along the length of the bowl. The curving fibres create a much stronger shape and a spoon which is going to last for generations rather than just thirty or forty years.

It is rare to find really old spoons in use, but when you do they inevitably tend to carry their story with them. Once, at a market in Stroud, I stopped to talk to an olive seller who was using what looked to be really old spoons. They turned out to have been made by the grandfather of a friend of mine who is also a spoon carver. I still carry spoons from my travelling days, including one made by a journeyman German carver with whom I did a spoon swap (he's a very accomplished cabinet maker now). My mother has spoons that I made as a teenager, and though looking at them now they are pretty unrefined, at the time

I was very proud of them. Handmade spoons always end up being an artefact of sorts.

A shovel-ended spoon such as this is obviously good for moving material around, but it is also good for flipping; it has a wide, flat surface useful for scraping, which is also wide enough for spreading. In short, this spoon is a really useful, practical shape. The large flat dome shape of the bowl is, however, an inherently weak shape if made from straight wood. This is because the short fibres can absorb water, changing shape over time and being prone to splitting. But by using the bent branch we achieve strength because the natural bend keeps the fibres running along the length of the bowl, and without open ends they absorb water much less readily.

The tool is also stronger when the fibres run straight out of the rim because the ends of the fibres that wear against the pan are supported in long bundles. As with the standard cooking spoon, strength at the rim is important, as cooking utensils tend to wear a lot on their leading edge. So, unlike the standard cooking spoon, with a bent branch we can achieve a rim with a sharper edge whilst remaining hard-wearing.

Consider carefully the angle of the crank, as you ideally want to be able to balance the end of the spoon's handle on the handle of the frying pan, so it clears the rim without touching it. You need to create enough crank to stop your spoon from burning on the edge of the pan if you leave it inside.

When creating a blank out of a bent branch, however, you need to be quite careful when splitting the wood as often bent branches have twists in them, which make them quite tough.

The split billet naturally gives us our flat shovel end, but we now need to give some shape to the back of the bowl. Axe

facets on both sides, from the flat end back down towards the handle to reveal the depth of the bowl. Deciding where the neck should come in is important to get right, and following this sequence really helps. Draw where the bowl best sits in these three dimensions, and with the aid of your guidelines axe away the handle. If where the neck naturally comes in makes the bowl too long, you may decide to saw a bit off the shovel end. Take the bulk of waste wood from the bark side down towards the bowl to complete the blank.

I think the sides of the spoon bowl look nicer if they are not perfectly parallel, so consider tapering them outwards. This aids the function of the spoon as it allows you to better scrape the sides of a flat pan and get into the corners.

Thinking about the spoon in cooking also affects how we shape the handle, which is a lot chunkier than those we find on mass-produced cooking spoons. Your handle should be fatter towards the middle so it jams tight in your hand whilst being used like a shovel. It is important that the end of the spoon is rounded and facetted, as you tend to use the spoon for scraping with your palm pressed on the end.

Roma Spoon

I may say this of many spoons, but this is really my favourite because of what it evokes. This is in part because of the Roma's roots in the artisan – this is a terribly overused word but here it has a huge impact upon the form of the spoon. Roma spoons are characterised by the broad, fast cuts and pronounced facets of the jobbing carver; they are designed to be made quickly for money.

The Roma is a good cooking spoon because the egg-shaped bowl gives you the point that you need to get into the corners of the pan. The egg shape is also a sensible and strong shape for a straight wood; the elongated front of the bowl is less prone to splitting from expansion/contraction when it gets wet and then dries out, and it has slightly longer fibres in the leading edge of the rim than in a circular bowl. And, unlike the leaf-shaped cooking spoon, it has the added benefit of being ambidextrous.

These spoons are made out of straight-grained wood, and in order to be quick and efficient you don't want to use too thick a piece of wood. Splitting the smallest possible bit of wood that you can make the spoon from means you have the least material to remove. This not only makes it efficient in terms of speed but also saves on materials.

To achieve the crank in our fairly thin bit of wood I like to have it quite far forward, so we look to have a distinctive 'bump' where the crank goes abruptly into the bowl of the spoon from the neck. A bump at this juncture gives the spoon extra strength, reinforcing the weakest part of the spoon, but it also allows you take more wood off the back – and removal of wood is what it's all about – which in turn allows you create a more shapely backside to the bowl.

When trying to create the crank in a spoon like this, it can be very helpful to saw into the neck and split the handle sides away. This gives a very accurate profile shape which makes cutting the crank easier. You could even saw down at the point where the bowl meets the neck to create a stop point to axe down towards. When carving the crank in these spoons you are aiming to create a flat surface to the top of the bowl, which goes from the tip of the bowl to the neck of the spoon.

To create the distinctive neck on these spoons, undercut the back of the bowl using the reinforced pull stroke to get into the neck of the spoon. It is then possible to ping the wood out with the grain, leaving you a sharp junction where the neck meets the back of the bowl, rather than a smooth curve. This technique can save a lot of time that is wasted going back and forth trying to create smooth tight curves.

Continue to take the neck in tight with a triangular cross section which then flattens out towards the end of the handle. Once the neck is neat and tidy from the bottom, you can give the illusion of delicateness by taking it in further from the top of the neck back towards the top of the bowl. This makes what was a triangular cross-section at the neck into a diamond shape. This technique creates a very organic feel and the stem begins to resemble the joints on an insect. This makes the spoon more delicate; but it's also strong.

Turned Spoon

This spoon is started with an axe to create a blank which has no crank and little shaping to the bowl. A lathe is then used to turn the handle and round the profile of the bowl, and then the back of the bowl is carved with a knife and hollowed with a spoon knife. Even though a beginner spoon carver perhaps won't have access to a lathe in the first stages of their interest, I wanted to include it here as a pole lathe is a beautiful and useful machine to use. I also think it is interesting because the vast majority of spoons bought from a supermarket are made on robot lathes in factories. This spoon shows how, with a very basic home-made lathe, we can produce something much more beautiful. Perhaps in the future, 'progress' will involve making more beautiful things this way.

Turning is a clever way of making things straight and creating a pleasingly smooth surface, and it's extremely quick to do. Some people are more impressed by a turned handle than a carved handle, but this is because most people do not understand that a facetted handle requires much more skill and effort on behalf of the carver.

You still need to rough out your spoon blank with an axe. This way you don't have to remove all of the wood with

a lathe. But when you make the blank, be sure not to shape the end of the bowl as this needs to be left with a large blunt end, so that the centres of the lathe can be slightly offset. This allows you to add a little crank to your spoon.

Turn the cylindrical handle of the spoon first. Interestingly, we also create the shape of the rim on the lathe. This is done by shaping the profile of the spoon rather than the back of the bowl. You need to have the lathe spinning reasonably fast, and a very steady hand with your chisel. This part of the process is satisfying because it gives us instant symmetry and makes for a very neat profile.

As an English spoon carver, I like to turn an acorn on the end of the handle, as it is the seed of the mighty oak. You can carve the surface of the acorn, which I leave slightly larger on the lathe, adding a few facets to the cup and distinguishing it with a few cuts after turning.

Take the spoon off the lathe and round the bowl forward. In doing so, remove the nobble from the bowl end entirely. Do this with your knife, then hollow out the bowl with a bent knife to finish the spoon.

8

Serving Spoons

Pouring
Ladle

Salad
Spoons

Bent Branch
Ladle

Sugar
Spoon

There is something very joyous in serving food to somebody and, for me, it produces very strong feelings associated with sharing and giving. It is a physical gift and something we all do, which is a way of caring for somebody and nourishing them.

Certain foods allow you to use your spoons in a very nice way. The curvature of a fantastic serving bowl with an undercut rim actually rolls the food on top of the spoon instead of having to chase it around the bowl. And there is something profound about ladling something voluminous and wet. Part of the joy of serving lies in the movement itself, the simple carriage of something from one place to another – in a similar vein I am captivated by the mechanical action of cranes, by the simple and somehow generous movements involved.

Once, while working in the woods, I had what you might call a 'spoon epiphany'. One lunchtime on a fine summer's day I found myself standing in a woodland, fishing eggs out of a big pan, which was boiling away on an open fire, with a beautiful turned spoon. I was suddenly touched by a sense of something inherently peaceful and generous in the act of serving these eggs. It may have been a reaction to a rather chaotic time I'd had in the years leading up to it, but this moment really came out of nowhere and confirmed that I was in a good place. It was a moment of pure clarity when I felt that everything was right.

Pouring Ladle

All ladles are really pouring ladles, but we can distinguish this one easily because it has a spout. This feature is my own addition, although the design is based on a spoon I first saw in a museum.

A few of my spoons are based on historical designs, and this one came out of a visit to Roy Stephenson, who is Head of Archaeological Collections at the Museum of London. At the time I was interested in finding out more about 'London spoons' and Roy suggested I see a Roman-era spoon.

This spoon is a celebration of the different surfaces you can create in wood. So you have a nice clean, flat surface to the handle, beautiful facets where the bottom of the bowl has been carved with a bent knife, and a series of subtle rings where the spoon has been turned on a lathe.

Creating the billets for these spoons is both neat and economical because you get two ladles out of the same piece of wood, like a yin and yang. Cut your log to length then split it in half. After sketching the rough shape of your spoons with a pencil, saw two cuts into the half log, one at each neck. This can now be split in half again to create our two asymmetrical spoon blanks. Taking one billet, rough

shape the back of the bowl with an axe before putting the spoon onto a lathe to hollow the bowl. You can then use the lathe to shape the outside of the bowl and hollow out the inside. For a bigger bowl like this, turning is a very efficient way of removing the material, rather than using a spoon knife, but there's no reason why you couldn't carve a similar shaped spoon using the axe, instead.

The handle is offset, so the whole spoon is asymmetric, like a '6', and so needs no crank in the traditional sense. You collect your food through rotation, dipping straight down and turning the spoon in, rather than trying to get underneath it. You can use these spoons for pouring or serving almost anything. They are very good for soups but could also certainly be used as a measuring scoop, and originally they may have come in many different sizes.

This one has a nice square hole at the top of the handle, which is quite straightforward to add. You could use a drill to make this hole, but as green wood workers interested in traditional tools it is more in keeping with our practice to use a knife. I also tend not to drill holes because you don't get such a nice surface. Take a chip out from both sides of your handle, using a knife with a tip. To do this, first mark out your hole with a pencil on both sides – the part of the handle you are chipping should be relatively thin – and do a couple of initial cuts to sever the fibres. You can then make repeated straight incisions, aiming to meet in the middle of the handle. You are carving blind, so the tip of the knife is hidden from you. It's wise to make the hole small in the beginning, because you can always enlarge it to tidy it up later on.

Salad Spoons

When I used to sell spoons on the street I would often refuse to make salad spoons. My customers tended to request a fork as the second part of a serving duo. 'I am a spoon carver!' I would protest. However, I have to concede that these spoons are most useful as a pair, and if making them you should be prepared to make a concession to the fork by making one utensil with a split in it. But I would still call this a spoon!

The issue with serving salads is essentially how to pick up large leaves. This is best done with your hands, but this is unseemly so we create our spoons essentially as prosthetics. These tools need to encourage a certain delicacy as you certainly don't want to dent your lettuce, but they also need to be able to drain a wet salad which contains tomato and olive oil. Some spoon makers talk about needing these spoons to be perfectly flat so that they fit together nicely as a pair, but I don't think this is so important. It's quite nice to have to chase your food around sometimes.

Make them the same way you do a standard cooking spoon, but look to craft them a fraction longer. You want to create a length which doesn't topple over or get lost in your lettuce, but it's really a question of working to the bowl you use to mix and serve your salad. For me, this means having them around a foot in length, but you can really alter them according to your needs.

The forked half of our duo of spoons is useful when straining oilier salads, and this fork is quite easy to create. Firstly, you need to put a hole into your fig-shaped bowl. However, this can make it quite weak and prone to splitting, so we need to pre-empt the split.

Make the hole in your spoon blank with a tightly curved spoon knife, or if you find it easier, use a drill. If you are drilling, it's best to do this early on whilst there is still wood to remove from the inside and outside of the bowl. A really sharp drill – preferably one with a spur on – is best as it leaves a nice finish. If using a spoon knife for the hole, finish the bowl first then make a small hollow from either side of the spoon with a much tighter spoon knife, until you have made a hole that is no larger than a medium-sized olive. From the hole you can then mark out a split with your pencil before using a fine saw or a knife to create it – despite the name this should be cut rather than split. You can then bevel down the edges of the split in your finished spoon.

I love the asymmetry of the growth rings in these spoons. I'm more interested in using grain like this than the much celebrated spalted wood or burrs. I like that it just uses everyday standard wood to make something more beautiful and actually makes the spoon stronger. When the growth rings line up this way the spoon tends to be slightly stronger than if it is on a perfect radius (with straight lines through the bowl), or a perfect tangent (with circles aligned symmetrically in the bowl). It's stronger because with the growth rings running obliquely through the bowl you get longer fibres, which hold together better than short ones. When I get the circles centred in the bowl customers are really impressed! But it doesn't take much skill. Of course, you have to be careful, but it's a bit like carefully folding a piece of paper perfectly in half.

Bent Branch Ladle

Here we use the bent branch in a really classic way, to give our spoon a very deep crank for getting into a deep pan. As opposed to other, smaller spoons, where we use the bent branch mainly to create a strong rim or a smooth bowl for your lips, here we also employ it to create strength in the neck of a big ladle.

You can stop the whole spoon from falling into the food with the addition of a hook, which is a lovely design feature of this spoon and also helpful for storage as it will probably not fit in a kitchen drawer. Think carefully about where your hook should be and position it according to the size of pan you wish to hang it on. You may also wish to consider where the hook needs to be in relation to where you wish to store the ladle in the kitchen. When creating your hook, one option is to use the tip of a knife to carve it out. The knife then allows you to get into the tight corners of the hook. The alternative is to drill a hole in the handle before whittling in your hook shape.

We need to consider the potential weakness that adding a hook could bring to our spoon. When flexing the handle, the weakest point is obviously going to be at the hook, but when I flex a spoon I like to be able to feel the strength

along the whole length and not be able to predict where it is going to snap. I own a bent branch eating spoon made from fast growing ash, so with a high flexible strength, which is very satisfying to flex and note how it has been carved in sympathy with the material.

We address the fact that we are effectively reducing the overall strength of the spoon by leaving extra material at the weakest point, above the hook. Do this by bevelling to create a smooth, facetted edge to the top of the spoon, much like the top of the feather spoon. This adds strength and also helps us to maintain the illusion of thinness on the sides, as well as the flat look of the handle. The challenge of carving a complex shape such as this is always going to be about trying to get all of your lines to marry up, to create the coherent shape you eventually want.

Sugar Spoon

This spoon is another of my favourites, in part because it is so very small. This means you cannot confuse its use. If the sugar spoon were to be any longer then people would also use it to stir their tea before putting it back into the bowl. A sugar bowl often has a lid on, to prevent bugs and dust getting in, and because this spoon is so short you can just leave it in the bowl, much like the caddy spoon.

I also love how economical this spoon encourages you to be with wood. This is a beautiful spoon to make if you are cutting down a small tree with small branches, as thin as an inch in diameter – with side branches, smaller still – which would otherwise be waste wood, even to the average spoon carver.

This is another spoon made from a bent branch. Birch is perfect for this spoon because it splits very nicely, and the fibres aren't too entangled in the knots at the bend. Take your birch sapling or branch and pick which little side branch is to become the handle. First saw along the line where this side branch comes into the larger one, then saw across the larger stem setting the length of the bowl. This will define how long the bowl will be from the twig handle. Using a saw with this size of spoon means there

is less chance of getting it wrong, much less so than if you were using an axe. So split the main branch in half across the pith; we can even leave the pith in the side branch – on something so small it shouldn't split.

Due to the bent branch, you get a really deep crank with this style of spoon which would be a hard work and very weak carved out of a small bit of wood. Because this spoon is so tiny, the crank-carving process would be extremely fiddly and dangerous to axe.

Shape the back of the bowl first into a roughly half cylinder shape; you can then hollow out the bowl, or scoop, straight with the grain. Using a small spoon knife will give you a nice clean finish as it will cut across the majority the surface in one shaving.

First make your handle square, as this makes it easier to fashion the ball on the end of the spoon. We want the ball, which will be an extremely ergonomic little twizzling nobble, to be a little bit smaller than a pea. You can then adjust the spoon by rolling the knobble between your forefinger and thumb.

To create the ball, firstly facet the end of the handle at 45 degrees. Then measure the length of the first facet by eye and mark the same length out on the body of the square handle. At this point, score into the handle all the way around, before bevelling in the bottom edge of the ball. We can then take off the square corners of the handle to create an ergonomic, octagonal shape.

If you like, you could leave a much longer side branch handle and make a more traditional bowl shape to make a lovely twig handle spoon with the bark left on. You can even do this on a much larger scale to create ladles with branch handles.

9

Eating Spoons

| Fig Shaped Spoon | Swedish Spoon | Cawl Spoon | Dolphin Spoon |

Making an eating spoon requires the carver to consider the sensuality as much as the functionality of the spoon; these are spoons which go into the mouth and so speak of the very intimacies of eating. As such, we need to consider foremost their softness in and out of the mouth, as well as what we might call the 'mechanics of eating' – whether the spoon will be used for supping or with solid foods, and whether it will be used in a bowl or on a plate.

The eating spoon needs to be the correct width for your mouth. I sometimes think about offering a bespoke, made-to-measure spoon fitting service, where people come to my shop for an hour and have their mouth measured; this is a dream scenario for me. I wouldn't use a crude kind of medieval-looking device. Rather, customers would be able to eat with several different spoons and we would work out the perfect spoon from there.

These spoons are perhaps best enjoyed used with a wooden bowl; the gentle thud the bowl makes as it hits the table and the soft wooden sounds of eating are infinitely more enjoyable than the clunk and clatter of metal forks on ceramic plates. A wooden bowl keeps the food warmer while insulating your hands from hot stew so you can cradle your bowl in your hands whilst you eat snug on your sofa.

These four eating spoons suggest the range of forms possible within the genre. The fig shaped spoon and the Swedish eating spoon are in some respects complete opposites, both in terms of their aesthetic and the methods you must use to make them, as this chapter will reveal.

Fig Shaped Spoon

This type of spoon is often referred to as a 'medieval spoon', and I discovered the spoon which inspired my design in a medieval collection at the Museum of London. Handling it was somehow a soothing experience, and noting the familiar techniques and aesthetic qualities made my own practice feel both timeless and relevant. It confirmed me as part of a tradition, that I have much in common with the medieval man!

I feel quite certain this style evolved alongside metal spoons, as to my mind they don't seem born purely from wood culture. This is the obvious form to make when working metal with a hammer. If you are using silver, for example, you just keep hammering the bowl until it comes to that round shape, and the handle naturally starts square then becomes octagonal – hammering on top with something underneath creates parallel lines in the lower part. It's easy to get eight surfaces in metal, and it's also easy to create this functional shape in wood.

The fig shape of this bowl has a beautiful organic form, just like a fig. The aim is to create a spoon which allows you to get a good mouthful without having to create an awkward depth to the spoon. You need a shallow curve to the hollow itself as your top lip is effectively going inside the spoon to pull the food out onto your tongue, so you don't want a steep sided bowl. This is a multi-purpose rather than a supping spoon, and not really designed for pouring liquid into your mouth.

As should be obvious, the major part of the hollow of the bowl is concave, but where it meets the rim at the widest point, where your lips are being stretched most and reaching into the depths of the spoon's bowl, you need the spoon to be convex towards the rim. This gives your lips an easier ride without the rim digging in to your lip. You should also look to thin your bowl towards the leading edge of the spoon, creating a gradient which goes from thick at the deepest part of the bowl to thin on the rim – this gradient helps your lips drift effortlessly from the spoon.

The curve to the top of the spoon helps to create the 'bump' I love so much, where the handle transitions into the bowl. The way this comes to a sharp ridge really accentuates the curve at the neck. We create the long, tapering handle by chopping, or even sawing, two cuts in at the neck before splitting the wood off along the fibres.

When creating a thin handle like this, it's really worth carving with the fibres. This makes it much stronger and it's also infinitely easier to carve. We have a gradual taper to the handle which means you should be carving 'downhill' all the time. This is good because it allows for predictable carving, where there's no need to keep flipping it around so the knife doesn't dig in.

As mentioned previously, the eight-sided handle is a functional, sensible form to create. Simply start with a crude, square, four-sided handle and then take the corners off with your knife, taking it to eight sides. This octagonal handle allows you to twizzle it in your fingers, like a pencil, which encourages dexterity in the eater – a dexterity we may well need to relearn in an age where people write on a laptop, or even a phone. I wonder whether we will adopt new spoon techniques for the digital age?

Swedish Spoon

The Swedish style in spoons is defined for me by a large shallow bowl and a short handle. When combined with a very steep crank, as we see in this eating spoon, the effect is a distinctive 'keel', much like the keel on a boat. The keel adds strength where the neck is thinnest and often where there may be short grain. This is also an aesthetic part of the composition – an artfulness which I build up by adding bold, clear facets. Pondering the possibilities of subtly combined function and effortless archaic beauty is the obsession of the spoon carver.

This is really a multi-purpose spoon which works very well in a bowl, but also on a plate because the spoon is so shallow. I frequently carve these spoons with shovel ends too. People often say that it looks like a porridge spoon, though I wouldn't want to pigeonhole it as such. That said, I do recommend using it to eat porridge, because slimier food comes off a wooden spoon very nicely, and it is good to get people hooked on eating with proper spoons.

We also achieve a radical crank angle by having a very large bowl and a very short handle. Be aware that if you try to add a long handle then suddenly your curve, which

is crucial to the look of the spoon, flattens out. Adding even a centimetre to your spoon handle can make a huge difference.

There are a number of effective illusions involved in the creation of this spoon. Aim for a shallower curve to the top of the bowl, which you can further accentuate by thinning down the bowl towards the front. When contrasted with the thickness at the keel, this gives the illusion of more crank. A tactical thickness and thinness, the suggestion of tight curves, gives you the dramatic movement which makes the spoon so pretty. Our next spoon also employs a sleight of hand in order to make a powerful visual impact.

Cawl Spoon

The way the cawl spoon is cut in at the neck is extremely beautiful and gives the perception or illusion of delicacy, as the lines here are very close together. This technique is the same as that used by fashion designers who make clothes out of striped material in an attempt to lead the eye to what they wish to accentuate.

The form of this spoon is tied intimately to its function as a tool for supping cawl, a hearty broth made with meat and root vegetables, one of the national dishes of Wales. So there's a definite technique to using it from the side rather than end on. Its side bowl, perfect for soups, makes it slightly more slurpy than other spoons.

The tradition of spoon carving in Wales seems to have endured longer than elsewhere in the British Isles, and the most famous example is of course the Welsh love spoon. These have now sadly become rather twee and cheesy, which is a shame because they are born out of a beautiful tradition. Early twentieth century Welsh love spoons are often slightly grotesque, with chains and balls and cages, and loaded with weird Victorian meaning. The older Welsh love spoon, which might have a heart or two people's initials on it, is much more beautiful, and part of a tradition of giving a carved spoon as a token of your love.

It is perhaps worth reflecting here that working in three dimensions allows you to tell a complex story, at times letting you baffle the viewer. In other words, you shove lots of information at a person and hope that they come away with a feeling, rather than a complete understanding. So the neck on the cawl spoon isn't as delicate as it appears. It suggests both strength and fragility, and for me, with this particular form, that illusion is almost the most fascinating thing.

The cawl spoon has a wide, lozenge-shaped bowl with a long and thin handle. Legend has it that the thin handle was designed to pierce it into the stacks of peat – an ancient fuel – with the cawl bubbling away on the fire behind. This may well be a myth, but you can well believe it from the arrow shape of the handle. I've even used spoons as tent pegs in the past, when I was a trampier kind of spoon carver and sleeping in a field when I couldn't find suitable sticks!

The thin handle is good for twizzling, because if used properly you are turning the spoon, finally tipping it with the wrist to finesse the soup into your mouth. The spoon also has a deep crank to help you get into the bottom of the sort of deep bowl you invariably use for broths.

Dolphin Spoon

This spoon is also reminiscent of an old Welsh implement. Indeed, the design was inspired by a spoon in Jonathan Levis' book *Treen for the Table*, where he suggests that dolphin spoons originally came from Caernarfonshire, where you can see dolphins off the coast. This is another elegant eating spoon and, just as other spoons in this book are inspired by human, animal or cultural elements, aspects of the design suggest the influence of marine forms.

What characterises the dolphin spoon is the elongated thumb tab – that distinctive flick of the tail which suggests the dolphin. In practice, the thumb tab/tail allows us to get quite a large crank out of a thin bit of wood. Because the tab comes out at a very steep angle, you hold it differently to other types of spoon, and it works very well if you hold it right on the end. Again, this is really a multi-purpose eating spoon, from an age when most people would really just have had one eating spoon. (I tell my customers that we now live in an age where you are allowed to own several.)

I use a fairly thin bit of wood to create the spoon and start by putting in quite an abrupt crank at the neck. In a technique unique to this spoon, we can also axe in from the tail end to create the thumb tab, cutting across the grain,

and splitting off the excess wood from there too. Don't make the tail too long or the spoon will be weak.

Aim to have the fibres of the wood running straightest at the joint of the neck and bowl, because this is going to be the weakest part. I like to make this style of eating spoon with quite a rounded, egg shaped bowl, and I use the *twca cam* to make the hollow, coming back from the tip towards the neck to give a really nice symmetrical curve.

I often create this spoon out of a banana-shaped bent branch – not a steeply bent piece we might value elsewhere, but rather a subtle bend which would give you more strength to the bend of the thumb tab itself.

The New Wood Culture

There are a few things I hope you'll take away from this book, from practical tips regarding the hands-on business of carving, right through to broader social, environmental and philosophical points. In my mind, however, these things are not really separable, or rather they are all joined up. This book represents a holistic approach to making spoons.

Perhaps now when using spoons, you'll take your time to exist in that moment of action, appreciating your own dexterity and skill with this most democratic of tools. This book is designed to encourage you to see the joy in the circular motion of a spoon in a mixing bowl, in the long slurp of soup poured with a tipping action from a ladle, and in the age-old chase of an olive around a salad bowl.

I hope that you will begin to note the importance of form, and how the shape of all tools affects not only how they work, but also how you feel when using them. Personally, I find that the more space I give my brain to pondering form, taking time to appreciate the details, the more rewarding it becomes.

The book is also about the efficiency and beauty of the most basic edge tools; perhaps I have suggested something of the depth of my own love of simply peeling shavings. Just a few edge tools and some simple wooden ones, like the mallet and wedge, which you can make yourself, are really all you need. For me, there is no need for noisy industrial machines, especially when you are working with green wood.

The safe and efficient techniques described here give you the control to shape fresh wood. From choosing the material right through to refining the rim of the bowl, the 'foundation skills' are relatively quick to acquire, but very hard to master.

I hope that the spoon carver will be inspired by the sixteen designs found in part three of this book; I wish I'd had a few of these documentary photos when I started out carving, to suggest the three-dimensional possibilities that exist with spoons. However, the spoons featured in this book are really just a starting point, and I sincerely hope that you will share images of some of your creations with me.

I have, of course, tried to suggest something of my own love of woodland, and to inspire you to care (and read more) about trees. Shouldn't we all know at least a dozen species of trees? Or how old an oak can grow? We should all strive to learn more about woodland management, grafting, tree spirits … At the very least we should learn how best to prune the neglected fruit tree in our suburban garden.

I happen to believe the world would be a better place if we all found out who owns our local woodland and who is managing it. If your local woodland seems neglected, then perhaps this book will prompt you to enquire if it might be better managed. If there is a local coppice worker, then support them by buying their products, or volunteer with a coppice group and get involved yourself. If you are lucky enough to own a field or two, then maybe you can fence out livestock and allow some woodland regeneration.

Most importantly you must get out there and make contact with real trees. In an age where a growing number of people are calling for us to turn away from oil culture, with our endless resource wars and the plastic now choking our oceans, I am proffering a new direction. Don't panic: I am not asking you to throw away your smartphone (though you could turn it off for the odd afternoon). Rather, an age where we are more connected to nature, sourcing energy where it is freely available from the sun and wind, and using materials sustainably harvested from diverse managed woodlands.

I suspect the greatest wood cultures are ahead of us, and I hope you may be part of getting us there. I for one, on any given summer's day, would certainly rather sit in the dappled shade of an old oak tree than the shadow of a barrel of oil.

Now get out there and make spoons!

Stockists & Resources

For spoons, tools, wooden blanks and video tutorials, visit my website: barnthespoon.com

And don't forget to share your adventures in spoon carving with me on Instagram @barnthespoon

For classes in spoon carving, woodwork and blade-smithing visit thegreenwoodguild.com

I also co-organise the world's first annual international spoon festival, Spoonfest. Meet other spoon enthusiasts and enjoy a range of workshops taught by the world's finest carvers. Find out more at Spoonfest.co.uk

My Spoonspiration

Jan Harm ter Brugge, the Dutch master of design. My little sugar spoon is based on my favourite spoon which he made and in his words is a 'little schoop'. houtvanbomen.com, @spooncarver

Fritiof Runhall is one of my greatest inspirations: he has had much to do with the way I feel about woodwork and has taught me many carving techniques. He teaches at the incredible Swedish craft school Saterglantan (saterglantan. com) and can often be found sharing his skills at Spoonfest.

Jarrod Stonedahl is an incredible American woodworker; he taught the world to make spoons with short handles again, and we were all better off for it. woodspirithandcraft.com, @jarrod_dahl

Jogge Sundquist – there is no better letter carver on the planet. His fun and folky spoons are fantastic. surolle.se, @surolle

Owen Thomas was the first in line of the long suffering apprentices. He bore the brunt of working with a

willfully awkward and slightly mental mastercraftsman –
the others have no idea how easy they got it! I taught Owen
in my shop and we worked on the Roman Ladle together.
owenthomaswoodcraft.com, @owenthomaswoodcraft

Robin Wood. Co-founder of our beautiful little festival
Spoonfest and maker of exceptional wooden bowls that
are the perfect companion of spoons. robin-wood.co.uk,
@robinwoodcraft

Tools & Suppliers

Ben Orford, benandloisorford.com
Del Stubbs, pinewoodforge.com
Nic Westermann, nicwestermann.co.uk
Robin Wood, robin-wood.co.uk
Woodland Craft Supplies, woodlandcraftsupplies.co.uk

Further Reading

Agate, Elizabeth (Ed.) *Woodlands: A Practical Handbook*
(British Trust for Conservation Volunteers, UK, 2002)
Rackham, Dr. Oliver *Trees and Woodland in the British
Landscape* (W&N, UK, 2001)
Levi, Jonathan and Robert Young *Treen for the Table*
(Antique Collectors' Club Ltd. reprint edition, UK, 2013)
Sundqvist, Wille *Swedish Carving Techniques* (Taunton
reprint edition, UK, 2013)
National Coppice Federation, ncfed.org.uk

Thanks to Elen for being an incredible editor, for understanding why it's important that we get proper hand carved wooden spoons in every household, and for making this book happen.

I would also like to thank my teachers. There have been many along the way that have made all the difference, whether in spoon carving, teaching me the correct way to shovel gravel, or parallel parking (thanks Dennis!). I'd like to say a special thanks to my parents, who have been teachers their whole lives. So glad you didn't force me into becoming an accountant or lawyer (though sometimes I think the money would have been nice).

Thanks to Ben my long-suffering ghost writer who made sense of my tangled thinking; Debi for taking beautiful photos; Liz for sorting through the copy; Ben G for the design, and all the people behind the scenes at Penguin who believed in the project.

To Ken, Terry and Paul at Tower Hamlets Cemetery Park for allowing us to take the woodland photos, and who epitomise the countless wonderful people I have met on my journey that have made it all possible and worthwhile.

To Cath my partner for being wonderful, and all my friends and family who are used to putting up with my spoon obsession.

There are many others who I would also like to thank; you know who you are.

10 9 8 7 6 5 4 3 2 1

Virgin Books, an imprint of Ebury Publishing,
20 Vauxhall Bridge Road,
London SW1V 2SA

Virgin Books is part of the Penguin Random House group of companies whose addresses can be found at global.penguinrandomhouse.com

Penguin
Random House
UK

First published by Virgin Books in 2017

www.penguin.co.uk

A CIP catalogue record for this book is available from the British Library

ISBN 9780753545973

Text: Ben Williams
Copyedit: Liz Marvin
Design: Ben Gardiner
Cover Design: Two Associates
Photography: Debi Treloar, assisted by Woody Holding
Styling: Marianne Cotterill

Colour origination by Alta Image
Printed and bound in China by Toppan Leefung

MIX
Paper from
responsible sources
FSC
www.fsc.org
FSC® C018179

Penguin Random House is committed to a sustainable future for our business, our readers and our planet. This book is made from Forest Stewardship Council® certified paper.